# RESEARCHES

RESPECTING

# AMERICUS VESPUCIUS,

## AND HIS VOYAGES.

BY

THE VISCOUNT SANTAREM,

EX PRIME MINISTER OF PORTUGAL, MEMBER OF THE INSTITUTE OF FRANCE, ETC. ETC. ETC.

TRANSLATED

By E. V. CHILDE.

BOSTON:
CHARLES C. LITTLE & JAMES BROWN.
1850.

CAMBRIDGE:
PRINTED BY BOLLES AND HOUGHTON.

# RESEARCHES.

## INTRODUCTION.

THE discovery of the New Continent, which we owe to the genius of Columbus, was a fact of the utmost importance, on account of the remarkable influence it exercised in developing the human intellect. It enabled Astronomy, Physics, Botany, and Mineralogy, to add greatly to their stores by means of new observations and numerous experiments; and to it the moral sciences themselves too have not been less indebted.[1] From the comparison also of new idioms, manners, customs and opinions, invaluable materials have been extracted for the history of man.[2]

Since that event more than three thousand works have been written upon the history and geography

[1] Ancillon, Description of the Revolutions of the Political System of Europe. Vol. i. p. 191, et seqq.

[2] Ibid.

of this vast portion of the globe, and upon the expeditions which took place between the years 1492 and 1540. Notwithstanding, however, this immense number of literary productions, and the minute investigations they contained respecting the leaders and dates of these early expeditions, this part of the history of the geography of the New Continent remained in great obscurity up to the commencement of the present century. Till then there was a multitude of problems concerning the history and geography of the New Continent, which the research of many learned men had failed to solve.

Certain authors had indeed sought to ascertain if the New World had been known to the ancients, while others occupied themselves with the same question either in the hope of tarnishing the fame of Columbus,[1] or with a view to investigate the causes and traditions which led him to the enterprise that immortalized his name; or, finally, for the purpose of proving that this part of the world was the famous Atlantis of Plato.

Thus, since the sixteenth century, a *savant* of immense erudition, the celebrated Las Casas is found discussing in his *History of the Indies* all the pas-

[1] Although the roundness of the earth, and the antipodes, are found in almost all the cosmographical treatises of the fourteenth century, it is well known that at the end of the fifteenth many persons were unwilling to admit them as facts, and sustained a contrary opinion for the purpose of opposing themselves to the voyage of Columbus. Libri, History of the Sciences in Italy. Vol. ii. p. 197.

sages, whether from ancient authors or from those of the Middle Age, which in his opinion exerted a powerful influence on the mind of Columbus.[1] Then Scherer, in 1777, made a collection of certain geographical fragments respecting the knowledge which the ancients possessed of the existence of a New Continent.[2] And later, that is, in 1783, Masdeu occupied himself also in bringing together the observations of ancient authors, such as Plato, Aristotle, Diodorus Siculus, Posidonius, Strabo, Seneca, Pliny, Saint Clement of Alexandria, Ælian, Apuleius and Origen, which bore upon the existence of a continent separated from ours by the great ocean.[3] Passages from these authors we have seen this learned Spaniard grouping in one mass, for the purpose of showing that their united testimony proves that from the time of Solon to that of Origen, and even for a much longer period, comprising nine centuries, the tradition of another continent than our own has prevailed among the nations of the old world. But, on the other hand, nothing which is met with in the works of Adam of Bremen,[4] Torfæus,

[1] General History of the Indies, 1559. An unedited MS. in the library of M. Ternaux. *Vide* chaps. 5 - 11.

[2] Scherer, Historical and Geographical Researches touching the New World.

[3] Masdeu, Critical History of Spain. Vol. iii. b. 6, p. 324, et seq. "Clement of Alexandria" is here substituted, by a mistake of the author, for Clement *of Rome*, to whom Masdeu refers.

[4] An author of the eleventh century, in whose work it is pretended that there are indications of America's having been visited in his time by the people of the north. But those who have put their faith in

Gottlob Fritsch, Daniel Victor, Erasmus Schmid, nor of Cassel of Bremen, tends satisfactorily to solve the question, whether the New Continent had ever been visited by Europeans.

We have, therefore, thought it perfectly useless to repeat what has been already said by others, or to criticize anew these passages, especially as one of the most illustrious *savans* of our day, (M. de Humboldt,) [1] has very lately entered into a discussion of the same.

Previously to the year 1825, the discussions which appeared concerning the New Continent were rather matters of mere erudition than historical treatises upon positive facts. But then was brought forth *one of the most important memorials of modern times*,[2] which shed a new light upon many points of the highest interest, and opened to the world documents, hitherto unedited, of great value, respecting the earliest stages of discovery of the New Continent. We here allude to the work of our very learned friend, M. de Navarrete,[3] which has brought to the acquaint-

this author forgot perhaps that he himself was completely ignorant of the geography of the Baltic; that he had doubts whether Russia had even been reached by this sea, and moreover reckoned Esthonia and Courland among the number of the isles. See his work *De Situ Daniæ.*

1 Critical Examination of the History of the Geography of the New Continent. Vol. i. p. 15, et seq.

2 See these expressions in the Critical Examination by M. de Humboldt. Vol. i. p. 15 of the Introduction.

3 Collection of Voyages and Discoveries which the Spaniards made by sea since the end of the fifteenth century.

ance of *savans* an enormous quantity of documentary matter and new opinions, by means of which may be entirely re-written a large portion of the history of the New Continent, as it was known to us before this important publication. Following the production of M. de Navarrete, came the interesting *Life of Columbus*, by Mr. Washington Irving; and not long ago, M. de Humboldt published the result of his erudite labors.

In 1826, M. de Navarrete having consulted us regarding the voyages which Americus Vespucius pretended to have undertaken at the expense of Portugal, this question, so important to the geographical history of the New Continent, from that moment fixed our attention, and we consequently communicated to the learned Spaniard a memoir, in which we ventured to express our opinion on the subject, such as he was pleased to introduce into his own work.

To this memoir we afterwards added numerous notes and considerable new matter, all of which are contained in the present volume, although we acknowledge that it was not in such a form they were originally intended to appear, but in a work superior in method and of greater extent. The kind reception, however, they met with from many *savans*, and particularly from the Geographical Society of Paris, together with the repeated applications which were made to us at different times by one of the greatest authorities in this branch of science, our learned friend and fellow-laborer the Baron de Walckenaër, decided us to collect the several detached pieces hitherto published in M. de Navarrete's work, and in the volumes of the Bulletin of the Geographical Society, and to make to them many additions, which, with the analytical table, are now for the first time given to the public.

We are quite aware, and feel bound to admit, that, according to the strict rules of historical criticism, the highest importance should be attached to those documents, and to the testimony of those authors alone, which belong to the first half of the sixteenth century. Neither were we at any time ignorant of the fact that this importance gradually diminishes in proportion to the distance at which we leave this epoch behind. But the impartial reader will doubtless acknowledge that, in a discussion of this sort, the opinions of critics and historians of a later date, when they bear upon the same subject, should be cited for examination. For in order thoroughly to appreciate the merits of a controversy, one ought to have before his eyes all that has ever been written on either side of it.

We have thought it necessary also to give all the bibliographical indications, and to point out the sources, whence is to be obtained a profound and accurate knowledge of the question. And if this method is not indispensably necessary to historical criticism, it is at least of vast utility, in our opinion, for a correct appreciation of the truth. So that, without being over anxious about the criticism to which we may expose ourselves, we have taken upon us to detail whatever historians, geographers, and *savans*, in great numbers, have thought and spoken relative to Vespucius and his voyages, in the conviction that those who read our book without partiality will feel obliged to us, for having spared them the trouble of new investigations in search of materials whereon to form an opinion for themselves. We fancied, besides, that, by confining ourselves to the testimony and documents beginning with the commencement of the sixteenth century, we might break the thread of the history of this controversy, which, we may venture to say, has endured since the time of Vespucius to the present day.

It is not without regret that we have occupied ourselves with this question in a controversial manner, we who, in all our works successively published in the course of twenty years, have always most carefully avoided every sort of disputation. Nevertheless, our convictions upon the subject we proposed to treat were profound, and unfortunately, no argument to alter them has as yet presented itself. We had, moreover, the firm assurance that a controversial discussion of points, which have not been sufficiently elucidated, is always a gain to science. And, indeed, it is impossible to gainsay the importance and utility of such a discussion, when one sees how little was known to Forster, a writer at the end of the last century, about the Cabots and their voyages, and how all that concerns these navigators has been cleared up and illustrated by the invaluable work of M. de Navarrete, and especially by the learned labors of Mr. Biddle.[1] Convinced then of this truth, we have not hesitated to take up the question of Americus Vespucius, and of the first epoch of the discovery of the New Continent. The result of our investigations we now submit to the judgment of the learned.

We cannot by any possibility incur the charge of national partiality in what we have said, for our pleadings are rather in favor of the incontestable rights of Columbus, of Hojeda, of Lepe, of Cabral, and of Pinzon.* We have mistrusted the authenticity of documents coming to us under the name of Vespucius, and have expressed the very slight faith with which we were inspired by narratives, upon certain subjects of great importance, ascribed to the Florentine navigator. And if any one will take the trouble to follow us attentively, he will acknowledge that we have not attacked every weak point and every doubtful problem which is to be found in the

[1] Memoir of Sebastian Cabot, with a review of the History of maritime Discovery, illustrated by documents from the Rolls, now first published. London, 1831.

* It must be borne in mind that the author is Portuguese. — Tr.

letters of Americus Vespucius, but that, on the contrary, our incredulity as to the claims of the Florentine is the result of the most thorough investigation. Yet, let this be as it may, we have preferred, as says a learned professor,[1] to *present as doubtful what is true, rather than as true what is doubtful.*

The reader will also perceive by many passages in this book, that we have not attempted to conceal the part which Italians took in the voyages and discoveries of the fifteenth, and particularly of the sixteenth centuries. If our convictions, derived as they are from a conscientious study of documents, have extorted from our pen any expression respecting Vespucius which may appear too severe, it must be attributed to the profound impression made upon us by the inconceivable injustice committed against the noble and dignified character of Columbus; and, moreover, be it remarked that in severity our observations upon the Florentine navigator fall far short of those employed by a great number of most learned writers, beginning with Las Casas, his contemporary, and ending with M. de Navarrete, of our day.

If this first portion of our literary task fails to give perfect satisfaction to certain critics, instead of complaining, we will say to them beforehand, in the words of Forster, that "it is the lamentable fate of the learned not to be able, with all their pains, to

[1] Ampère. Literary History of France. Vol. i. Introduction.

obtain the information they would wish with respect to all the objects of their researches." [1]

There are other points, however, that we will attempt to discuss in the second part of our work, for the prosecution of which we have succeeded in amassing an immense quantity of materials.

We cannot close this introduction without expressing the most hearty gratitude to our very learned friend, M. Jomard, for the zeal and kindness with which he has had the goodness to place at our disposal many volumes of his rich and valuable library, besides a great number of materials for cartographical purposes, which are found collected in the precious depository of plans and charts in the Royal Library, — a collection of literary treasures increasing in value every day, thanks to the enlightened and untiring zeal of its able and learned founder.

M. Ternaux-Compans ought also here to receive a token of our lively gratitude for the instructive liberality with which he has spread before us the sumptuous stores of his splendid American Library. And with such aids as these it has been that we have succeeded in accomplishing a new and critical treatise upon the history of one of the most memorable and most fruitful discoveries which the human race has ever witnessed.

[1] Forster, History of Voyages and Discoveries in the North, (London, 1786,) p. 427.

## CHAPTER I.

NEITHER in the original chancelleries (*Chancellarias originaes*) of the king Don Manuel, from 1495 to 1503, inclusive, nor in the 82,902 documents of the chronological-records, (*Corpo chronologico*,) or the 6,095 of the chest-records, (*Corpo das gavetas*,) nor yet in the numerous letters missive from kings, princes, and other personages,—letters deposited in the royal archives, have we found the slightest mention of the name of Vespucius, or of those of Giuliano del Giocondo and Bartolomeo del Giocondo.

We ought to add that we have never encountered the name of Vespucius in the exceedingly valuable collection of manuscripts belonging to the royal library of Paris, which we examined during our stay in that city, which furnished us with materials for our critical memoirs published in volumes XII. XIII. and XV. of the *Annales des Sciences*, and which Balbi speaks of in the second volume of his *Essai Statistique*, when treating of literary archives. Neither is any mention made of his name in the manuscript, No. 10,023, entitled, *Journal des Voyages des Portugais, depuis l'an* 1497 *jusqu'en* 1632, a manuscript originally composed in Portuguese by a native of Portugal, and evidently taken from ancient memoirs, as appears from the orthography and double letters, which are still preserved.

One should regard, then, as extremely suspicious the pretensions of Vespucius, and place very little faith in all he says in his letters to Piero Soderini, which were translated into Portuguese and published in 1812, by the Royal Academy of Lisbon, in its *Collection of Notes relating to the History and Geography of the People beyond the Sea.* Our opinion, thereupon, has in no way changed, notwithstanding that of the learned Portuguese editor, who pretends, "that Pedro Alvares Cabral, returning to Portugal, where he arrived in 1501, encountered, in passing Cape Vert, a squadron of three vessels, in which was found Vespucius, who conversed with him." It is probable that the editor extracted these lines from a passage in the twenty-first chapter of a memoir upon the voyage of Pedro Alvares Cabral, written by a Portuguese pilot, and to be found in the third number of the second volume of the Collection above cited. This is the passage: "We reached the Cape of Good Hope on Palm Sunday; the wind being favorable, we doubled the Cape, and touched at a place, near Cape Vert, called *Besenegue*, where we found three vessels, which the king of Portugal had sent to reconnoitre the new land that we had discovered on our way to Calcutta."

How can any one believe that the name of Vespucius was so obscure as to escape being mentioned by the Portuguese pilot in his narrative? Because Cabral met these three vessels, does it follow that this was the supposed expedition of Vespucius, notwithstanding the coincidence of his first letter with the passage we have quoted? And hence to draw any affirmative conclusion in favor of Vespucius, is it not to make forced inductions of a most unsatisfactory nature? In our judgment, this said passage is not a proof of sufficient authority to supply the absence of written documents, and to induce us to put entire credit in the letters to Piero Soderini.

On the other hand, it is incredible that Damiao de Goes, a Portuguese historian *living at the time of these discoveries and voyages*, a man, too, of the greatest learning and of undoubted faith, whose stores of knowledge were prodigious, and who, after having travelled throughout Europe, became chief of the Royal Archives at the *Torre do Tombo*, where he left nothing untouched which could aid him in composing his Chronicle of the King Don Manuel; it is incredible that he who did not forget to speak of Pietro Pascoaligo, Venetian ambassador at Lisbon, in the sixty-second chapter of the first part of his work, never thought of mentioning the name of so celebrated a personage as Vespucius, while in every page he talks of other very indifferent persons; and that too when alluding, in the sixtieth chapter of the first part of the same Chronicle, to the return of Pedro Alvares Cabral, and to his arrival at Cape Vert, he briefly says: "And thence, he (Cabral) went to Cape Vert, where he encountered Pedro Dias, who separated from him in the pursuit of his voyage to the Indies, as we have above remarked." How is it possible to imagine that this author knew nothing of the pretended meeting of Cabral and Vespucius?

Damiao de Goes, during his residence at Padua, maintained the most intimate relations with Julio Sprone and other learned individuals; he interested himself greatly, too, in the voyages undertaken by the Portuguese at that time, and so familiarly acquainted with the subject had he become, that, on his departure for Holland, his Italian friends never ceased to consult him, and he it was who sent to Ramusio the manuscript work of Father Luiz Alvares. Nor is it possible for me to believe that this learned Portuguese historian, who was ignorant of no circumstances attending the voyages of Cadamosto, as is evident from the eighth chapter of the Chronicle of the Prince Don Joao, although not his contemporary, should just happen to know nothing of Vespucius's expedition.

How can it be supposed that Damiao de Goes was ignorant of the discoveries which Vespucius in his letters to Piero Soderini pretends to have made, when, after having visited Milan, Lombardy, Rome,

Ferrara and Venice, he became acquainted with a great number of *savans* in all these places, and maintained a literary correspondence with the cardinals Bembo, Bonamico, Sadoleto, Cristoforo Madruccio, John Magnus, his brother Olaus Magnus, and many other distinguished personages?

On his return to Portugal, Damiao de Goes, by an order dated June the 3d, 1548,[1] and signed by Don Joao III. was appointed chief of the royal Archives of the Torre do Tombo, as a reward for his services. He then engaged with great zeal in collecting all the materials necessary for the composition of the Chronicles which he afterwards published, and in properly arranging all the documents under his care. Is it then within the range of possibility that the voyage, and consequent renown of Vespucius, could have remained unknown to him, if indeed *this voyage had really taken place only forty-five years before?* Is it permissible to believe that Damiao de Goes would have met with no traces of these voyages; that he, who in the course of his travels had amassed a great quantity of manuscripts and rare documents, which were sent by him to the Infant Don Fernando, Duke da Guarda, and son of the King Don Manuel, would have found not a single one relative to Vespucius, if any such had existed?

Let no one pretend that Damiao de Goes, preju-

[1] Chancellery of the King Don Joao III. Book 60th, leaf 43.

diced in favor of his own countrymen, purposely kept silent, that he might obscure the glory of Vespucius, because Vespucius was a foreigner; for to Portugal already belonged the honor of this discovery, which was made by Pedro Alvares Cabral, the year preceding the date of Vespucius's hypothetical voyage ; in addition to which, Damiao de Goes was a historian of undoubted integrity, and his narrative of the voyage of Cadamosto, a foreigner as well as Vespucius, was written with the utmost impartiality.

How could it have possibly happened that the chief of the royal Archives knew nothing of the books and papers of Vespucius, when at the end of his compendium the latter says: "As soon as he had arrived in Portugal, he presented to the King, Don Manuel, his books and papers, which his Majesty desired to see and examine ?" [1]

We ought to remark also, that we have ourselves seen a letter, written by Pietro Pascoaligo, Venetian Ambassador at Lisbon, to his brothers in Italy, dated the 23d of October, 1501, the very year of Vespucius's imaginary voyage, and that while the writer speaks of the expedition of Cortereal, he makes not the slightest allusion to Vespucius, who was, like himself, Italian.

[1] Can it be believed that the King Don Manuel, who occupied himself so zealously in reforming the documents in the Archives, as to go in person to the depository of the Torre do Tombo, forgot to collect the books and papers which Vespucius speaks of, if indeed they existed, and neglected to have them copied, when they concerned an affair of such importance to his reign?

Besides, we have examined with attention those sections of our *Records of public diplomatic law in Portugal*, which treat of our national relations with Spain and Italy, and in none of them is to be found any thing respecting Vespucius. Ruy de Sande, too, Don Manuel's Minister in Spain, says not a single word of this Florentine in his despatches, written during 1500 and 1501, precisely the years in which Vespucius made his pretended discoveries, nor does Joao Mendes de Vasconcellos in his official correspondence of 1502, and the years following, ever make mention of his name.[1]

Neither Goes, nor the manuscipt in the royal Library at Paris, which we have already quoted, speaks of any important expedition in 1501, although they both allude to a voyage undertaken in that year by Joao da Nova, a very insignificant navigator when compared to Vespucius. And in this we find fresh cause for doubting the reality of the voyage and discoveries imputed to the latter.

As to his second voyage, Damiao de Goes says literally nothing, while other writers on the subject vary greatly in their narratives. Pedro de Mariz,

[1] We will add that at the epoch spoken of, it was the custom of our kings, either directly or through their ambassadors, to communicate all the remarkable events of the day to foreign monarchs, and especially to him of Spain, on account of family alliances existing with that sovereign. In these correspondences of the time, not having found any thing touching Vespucius or his discoveries, we are led still further to discredit the stories of the Florentine.

in his fifth dialogue, observes, without, however, indicating the year, "That the King Don Manuel sent a squadron of six vessels, commanded by Gonçalo Coelho, and that the captain, after having lost two out of the six, returned with the rest to Portugal, where he arrived subsequently to the death of the King."

Father Simao de Vasconcellos and several other chroniclers give the same account, but Damiao de Goes, in his chronicle, states in precise terms that Gonçalo Coelho departed with six vessels the 10th of June, 1503. If we could but recover the work of this Portuguese captain upon America, which he wrote by order of the king, after having himself personally ascertained the truth, we might be able to form a correct idea of the voyage of Coelho, and decide also as to the part which Vespucius took in it. But unhappily it is lost, and the only tradition respecting it which has reached us is, that its author presented it to the king, Joao III.[1]

We have likewise inspected in the Royal Archives of the Torre do Tombo all the documents concerning Gonçalo Coelho, and the genealogical memoirs of his family, and in none of them do we find any thing about Vespucius.

[1] But supposing that Vespucius actually shared in this expedition, the facts that Gonçalo Coelho was charged with the command, and wrote the history of it, are they not quite sufficient to destroy his exclusive pretensions to the discoveries claimed by him, and to deprive him of the glory of having his name given to these regions?

We should moreover add that the Florentine, speaking in his first letter of his arrival in the port of Besenegue near Cape Vert, makes not the slightest allusion to his rencounter with Pedro Alvares Cabral.

All that we have said demonstrates that the pretensions of Vespucius have very little foundation in truth, and that many historians and geographers have been led into error respecting him. And this can be shown in a manner still more clear by comparing different passages in his own writings. Is it not a contradiction, when, after having described in his first letter his voyage of 750 leagues of coast, he says: "that not having found in this country any mines, &c. &c.," and finishes, speaking always in a collective sense; and afterwards remarks; "*Thus it was decided, I being charged with the sole command of the squadron*"? Whence we must conclude that on first quitting Lisbon, he was not in command. Further on he adds: "We agreed with the first captain to make the signals to the squadron, &c. &c."

After the exposition we have made, and after the documents published by the Italians respecting Vespucius, it is our opinion that the discoveries to which he laid claim have a very slight foundation, and at the best are extremely doubtful.

To gain full and entire credit for a fact, criticism in our day demands proofs, the truth of which cannot be called in question. It is no longer satisfied with simple tradition, and discards documents whose character is worse than doubtful. Nevertheless, without a more thorough and profound examination of the subject, we will not venture to assert that Vespucius was in neither of these expeditions, as a navigator and cosmographer one of the most skilful; and notwithstanding all that he wrote, we are greatly inclined to adopt the opinion of the learned Muñoz. In a word, we should believe, (that is, if we are to regard his letters as genuine,) we should even believe that he really did share in both these, though only as a subaltern, and on that supposition our astonishment ceases at his having acted towards Portugal, and in respect to the voyages of 1501 and 1503, as he had already done in regard to the narratives of Hojeda.[1]

In order to have an opinion more decided on this question, we should have been much pleased had we

[1] It is proved that Vespucius, having got possession of the narratives of Hojeda, brought them out as his own. Koch, in his List of Revolutions in Europe, (vol. i. page 298,) says: "A Florentine merchant, by name Americus Vespucius, followed closely on the footsteps of the Genoese navigator, under the guidance of a Spanish captain, called Alonso de Hojeda. He made a number of voyages to the New World, visited several coasts of the South American continent, and in the maps of discoveries which he drew up, he arrogated to himself a glory which was not his due, by giving his own name to a new continent, whence it happened that this name, the name of America, has been constantly applied to that country ever since."

Wid-Tozen, cited by Koch in the fourth note of the same volume, and the page before mentioned.

been able to consult a work in German, published in 1823, and entitled, *Allgemeine Geschichte Neuerer Zeiten*, etc., " A general History of Modern Times," by M. Rotteck. We have met with only some extracts from this publication, but we remark that the author, in his inquiry whether America had ever been known or visited before the time of Christopher Columbus, speaks a great deal of Vespucius, and of the important part in this discovery he is made to play by certain writers, and adds this observation: " That which wars still more against the glory of Columbus is the pretensions of Vespucius." From which passage one infers that the author did not put much faith in Vespucius's narrations.

## CHAPTER II.

In the previous Chapter we have stated certain facts, and given our opinion respecting Americus Vespucius; and we have produced a great many contemporary or original proofs, which are, and which ought to be, good authority in the matter. Now we are going to group about our own opinion the opinions of several other writers, who have spoken of Vespucius, and have discussed the title of this Florentine to stamp his name upon the New World, at the expense of Columbus, of Cabral, of Gonçalo Coelho, and of others, and even to the prejudice of the important question, whether America had been known to the ancients. But before reviewing these opinions, we will here still further develop what has been asserted in a preceding page, that we have never found Vespucius's name even mentioned in any of the records of royal documents in the archives at Lisbon. And it is very remarkable, be it observed, that not only are the documents of the collections, exceeding one hundred thousand in number, which we have consulted and cited, perfectly silent in respect to him, but also that the registers of maps belonging to king Emmanuel are equally so. For Vespucius in his first letter to Piero Soderini says that, "*Being at Seville, intending never to return into Portugal again*, a messenger express, *with letters patent*[1] from the aforesaid seignior (the king Emmanuel) reached me," &c. &c. Letters patent from our kings were enregistered at the chancellery of the kingdom; and these registers, and the books containing them, are all in the royal archives of the Torre do Tombo forming a collection of more than two thousand volumes. Now, not a single one of these volumes is missing, so that the chancellery of the king Emmanuel is complete. How then could Vespucius have received *letters patent*, as he pretends, without their having been enregistered at the chancellery, according to the codes and laws? Is it to be presumed that the authorities were willing to violate these codes and laws in favor of Vespucius?

We will add to what has been said in another page, even at the expense of repetition, that Vespucius himself, in his letters to Soderini, establishes in the clearest manner that he was not at the head of the commission of discovery. For in another passage of his second letter he says: "*But our chief captain, a presumptuous and fantastic man, wished to go and reconnoitre, &c.*," — "*and to show him-*

[1] See the collection entitled: *Concerning Africa*, by Leo Africanus, and the Navigation of Ancient Portuguese Captains to the Indies. Translation of Jean Temporal, vol. ii. p. 477.

*self in the capacity of captain, he who was, nevertheless, in spite of all our other captains, &c.*"[1]

This passage, and this formal avowal of Vespucius himself, do they not prove that if perchance he belonged to the expedition, it was only as a subaltern; that the other five captains had as much right to give their names to the continent they visited as he; and that the commander-in-chief, in imposing his own upon it, possessed a much higher title than any of them?

In our preceding chapter we have not cited the authority of the historian John de Barros,[2] neither that of the classic Osorio,[3] both of whom were contemporaries of Vespucius, and authors worthy of high commendation, according to the universal esteem of *savans* in Europe. We will here produce whatever we have been able to draw from the two authentic sources touching the matter in hand.

Barros, in his treatise upon the discovery of Brazil, wherein he gives with most scrupulous accuracy the names of the captains who commanded vessels in Cabral's expedition, says not a word of Vespucius,[4] nor of his voyage in 1497, which is cited by several

[1] See the work before cited, page 492.

[2] Barros, born at the end of the fifteenth century, and lived in the time of Vespucius.

[3] Osorio, born at the beginning of the sixteenth century, and several years before the death of Vespucius.

[4] Barros, chap. 2, book 5.

geographers. And speaking of Columbus, this celebrated historian preserves a common silence with others, in regard to the pretended rencounter at Cape Vert with the ships, in one of which Vespucius is said to have been. He mentions only the meeting with Pedro Dias.[1]

As to the hypothetical voyage of Vespucius in 1501, this contemporary historian recounts no other departure from Lisbon but that of Joao da Nova, who set sail with four vessels in the month of March, 1501. And though he in no way conceals that this commander was not a Portuguese, no *allusion whatever is made to Vespucius.* When, therefore, he recorded the name of one foreigner, what motive could have influenced him to suppress that of another, if indeed that other, distinguished as was Vespucius in certain respects, had really taken part in the voyage of discovery, which was made at that epoch by order of the king? If this voyage of Vespucius had ever had an existence, would not Barros have mentioned his name, just as he has mentioned that of another Florentine, Ferdinand Vinet, among the captains who were in the command of vessels? What interest could he have had to conceal the name of Vespucius, and to say that *Ferdinand Vinet, a Florentine, commanded the ship, which was owned by Bartholomew Marchioni, likewise a Florentine?*[2]

[1] Ib. Decad. i. Book 5, chap. 9.

[2] Barros says that this Florentine resided in Lisbon.

This historian, so minute in historical details, has not confined himself to saying that one of the vessels was commanded by a Florentine and belonged to a Florentine, but he adds that the proprietor of it, Marchioni, resided at Lisbon. Is it then to be presumed that Barros, who was so well informed about all the fellow-countrymen of Vespucius residing at Lisbon, and engaged in navigation, could have been ignorant even of the existence of such a man?—that he should have known nothing of his having been called upon by the king, as his own story runs, a story repeated by so many geographers?

Nor is Vespucius less unfortunate in the testimony which this contemporary historian offers as to his pretensions respecting a second voyage in 1503.

Barros barely mentions a single expedition which was sent to India that year by the king Emmanuel. It consisted of three divisions, severally commanded by Alfonso de Albuquerque, Francis de Albuquerque, and Antonio Saldanha; but not a word is said by him of any enterprise of Vespucius, nor even of the place where he happened to be at that time.

Osorio,[1] a celebrated historian, of whom Lenglet du Fresnoy, in his work called, *The Method of studying History*, remarks, that his book is not only extremely well written, and held in high esti-

[1] Hieronymo Osorio.—Concerning affairs which were conducted under the power and auspices of Emmanuel, King of Lusitania, (Portugal,) Libri xii. Olyssipone, Antonius Gondisalvus, 1571.

mation, but that it is one of the choicest specimens of *historical composition for centuries past*, Osorio, in that part of his volume which treats of the discovery of Brazil, and of the voyages to that part of the world at the same period, describes only the expedition of Cabral and Gaspar de Lemos, without referring in any way to Vespucius. Can it be imagined, then, that this contemporary historian, who travelled in France, and much more in Italy, (for the purpose of acquiring the Eastern languages,) at an epoch when voyages and discoveries were the principal occupations of men's lives; that, if they had ever taken place, he could have been ignorant of the two voyages of Vespucius in 1501 and 1503, undertaken, as is pretended by the Florentine, in obedience to the king Emmanuel, whose history Osorio himself wrote? Or can it be believed that this author, so highly accomplished, never became acquainted, during his residence in France and Italy, and after his return to Portugal, with the numerous works already published respecting Vespucius in the two former of these countries as well as in Germany? Without question, they were all known to him, but as a faithful and conscientious writer he did not choose that any thing save truth should enter his history.

If, however, on the one hand, error and confusion were propagated by the letters of Vespucius and numerous productions akin to them; on the other, there appeared documents in many contemporary collections, which support, not only the Portuguese writers of that epoch, Barros, Goes, Osorio, and others, but also the opinion which we ourselves have formed. These are such as are found in a little book printed at Paris in 1516, in Gothic characters, and entitled, "*The New World and Voyages made by Americus Vespucius.*"

This small volume is nothing but a compilation of different voyages. It begins by a notice of those made by order of the Infant Don Henry, of Portugal, and of those of Columbus. Then follows a letter from Vespucius to Lorenzo de' Medici. But when it gets as far as the discovery of Brazil, in the sixth voyage, according to its calculation, it speaks of the discovery of Cabral, and we then have "*a copy of a Chapter of the Letters of Domenico Cretico, envoy of the Venetian Lordship in Portugal.*" In one of these letters, dated June 27, 1501,—the year in which Vespucius says he made a voyage by order of the king Emmanuel,—the Venetian commences by referring to Cabral's expedition, saying, that his government must have been already informed through its ambassador of that which the king had sent to India, and yet he relates that the said expedition, by quitting its prescribed course, had discovered *a terra firma, inasmuch as that by following the coast for more than five hundred leagues there was no end found to it*, &c., &c."

This Venetian agent was with the king Emmanuel at the moment of the squadron's return to port, and took part in the fêtes. He says, "*Being in company with the king when it arrived, I was sent for by him.*" And he adds, that his Majesty *advised him* to communicate the facts to his government. He then speaks of the return of a vessel, which was owned by one Bartholomew, a Florentine, but not a hint does he let drop either as to Vespucius or his expedition.

The Bartholomew spoken of, was, without doubt, the Florentine Bartholomew Marchioni, referred to by the historian Barros, as we have above seen. How then could have this Venetian diplomatist, who was an eye witness of all these transactions, who made an official report of them to his own court, and who had been admitted to the intimacy of the king Emmanuel, how could he have known nothing of the name of Vespucius, and of his pretended voyage at that epoch, when he does not omit to speak of another Florentine who played only a very inconsiderable part in these expeditions.

But, at the period we are now speaking of, the numerous copies and translations of Vespucius's letters, published in Europe, and particularly a work already quoted by many writers, — "*Introduction to Cosmography, respecting the four Maritime Expeditions of Americus Vespucius,*" printed in Lorraine, 1507, were the cause of this universal confusion of opinions concerning the voyages of the Florentine.

Most of the geographers living at the termination of the sixteenth century, as well as those of the seventeenth, spread still more widely this confusion, without ever giving themselves the trouble to investigate facts. This appears not only from many works and collections of voyages referred to by Bandini, Washington Irving [1] and M. de Navarrete,[2] and especially from those of Apian, of Vadianus and of Camers, quoted by M. de Humboldt,[3] but also from others, some of which we intend to enumerate.

Ruscelli, a celebrated Italian who was born at the commencement of the 16th century at Viterbo and died in 1566, added thirty-six new maps, both of the world known to the ancients and of the New World, to the geography of Ptolemy (Venice, 1561,) when he translated it. And although he gives the name of *Terra-Nova* to South America in his chart of that country, we find in an annexed article that he ascribes the discovery of it to Vespucius. But Cellarius did not wholly and exclusively adopt the pretensions of Vespucius and his panegyrists at the expense of Columbus's reputa-

[1] A History of the Life of Christopher Columbus. Paris, 1828.

[2] Navarrete, Collection of Voyages, vol. iii.

[3] Humboldt, A Chronology of the most ancient Maps of America. Bulletin of the Geographical Society, vol. iv. p. 411.

tion; for in his *Geographia Nova*, &c. (page 663) he says: — "*America, or Western India, was discovered by Christopher Columbus, a Genoese, in* 1492."

Certain geographers, however, of the 17th century, and among others, Baudrand,[1] had already begun to question the accuracy of the stories about Vespucius's discoveries, which were currently reported. Baudrand, in the article of his Geographical Dictionary entitled *America*, when speaking of Brazil, mentions the discovery of Cabral alone, although this he fixes at 1501 instead of 1500; but not a word does he utter regarding Vespucius, nor of his voyages in 1501 and 1503, said to have been undertaken by order of the King Emmanuel. Nevertheless he describes the New Continent as having been discovered by Columbus in the years 1492 and 1493, and afterwards by Americus Vespucius, who gave to it his own name.

Barlæus, in his work upon Brazil, written in Latin and published at Amsterdam in 1647, after having declared Columbus to have been the first discoverer of the New World, was deluded into the same error, with respect to Vespucius, as were the writers of the preceding century, and asserts that this Florentine discovered another portion of the New Continent under the orders of the king of Portugal.

[1] Dictionnaire Géographique, Amsterdam, 1701. Baudrand, born at Paris, 1633, died 1700.

The Historical and Cosmographical Dictionary of Juigné-Brossinière must have contributed still more to this confusion. And the author of it commits another and yet graver error in the following words: "Americus Vespucius, a Florentine by birth, having received the appointment of pilot, and enjoying the patronage of Emmanuel, King of Portugal, in 1407 [1] discovered the southern and western Indies, for which cause the New World was called America." Yet in the face of this enormous blunder, under the article *Brazil*, it is stated that this part of the New Continent was discovered by Cabral.

If in the eighteenth century the same errors have been continually adopted and propagated by certain authors and geographers, such as Bruzen de la Martinière,[2] the Benedictine Don Joseph Vaissette,[3] in his *Historical and Ecclesiastical Geography*, the authors of a *Geographical and Historical Dictionary of Italy*,[4] and Robinet, in his *Dictionnaire Universel*, it must be

[1] 1407. This date corresponds neither with the reign of King Emmanuel, nor with the epoch of a single discovery made in the New World. (Edition of 1644.)

[2] Dictionnaire Géographique, Historique et Critique.

[3] Géographie Historique, Ecclésiastique et Civile, printed at Paris, 1755. This author, however, says it was Columbus who first discovered America.

[4] This dictionary was published at Paris in 1775. The authors, or rather the compilers, have pursued a much more convenient course, by stating in the article *Vespucius*, that it is a matter of uncertainty whether Columbus or Vespucius was the first discoverer of America, &c. &c.

added that there are other writers, more conscientious as well as more learned, who have not fallen into them.

Of these we will mention several: Pluche,[1] after having spoken of Columbus, says, "Americus Vespucius, a Florentine navigator, who visited the same coasts of southern America, imposed upon the public to such an extent by his narratives, that the name of this adventurer was given to that whole country, when it would have been more just and natural that it should have borne that of Columbus, who was the first to discover the Isles and *Terra Firma*, or the Continent."

Charlevoix, eminent as he was, not only on account of his vast literary acquirements and erudition, but for his extensive travels, after having visited Italy, remarks, in his *Histoire Générale de la Nouvelle France*, that "Americus Vespucius had the honor of imposing his name upon the New World only by the aid of trickery." This industrious writer, in his *Tastes Chronologiques*, makes mention of no other expedition in 1500 save that of Cabral, and does not in the slightest manner allude to the two hypothetical voyages of Vespucius in 1501 and 1503. Referring to that of Hojeda in 1499, he says: "Americus Vespucius, who was nothing but a common personage in the squadron which Hojeda commanded, published a narrative of this discovery, assuming to himself the

[1] Concordance de la Géographie de différens Ages, p. 106.

honor of it; and in order to convince the public that he was the first European who ever touched the continent of the New World, he pretended that his voyage was of the duration of twenty-five months. To all of which, Hojeda, when judicially interrogated, *gave the lie direct.* (But the bare word of Vespucius having been at first trusted to, it became the custom to apply his name to the New World, and hence error at length prevailed over truth.") Charlevoix has added to his work a list, and a critical examination, of eighty-one authors whom he had consulted, and therefore it seems to me that he ought to be received as authority in this matter.

Lafitau, who for many years was engaged in making researches upon America, ascribes the discovery of this part of the globe to Columbus, and that of Brazil to Pedro Alvares Cabral.[1] This writer, who recounts only the voyages of Joao da Nova and Pedro Coelho, in 1501,—the year of Vespucius's imaginary expedition under royal auspices, preserves the most complete silence as to the latter person, nor does he so much as let slip a single word about his voyage of 1503.

Such is the profound silence of Lafitau upon Vespucius, that in the preface of his history, where he takes into consideration all the authors and manuscripts upon the voyages of the Portuguese, to be

[1] Histoire des Découvertes et des Conquêtes des Portugais dans le Nouveau-Monde. Paris, 1733. Vol. i. pp. 122, 123.

found in his time, and all of which were consulted by him, when speaking of the narratives and collections of Ramusio, he takes no notice either of Vespucius or of his letters, although some of these are to be found in the collections which he quotes.

The Abbé Raynal,[1] in narrating the discovery of Brazil, attributes it to Pedro Alvares Cabral alone, in 1501, without referring in any manner whatsoever to Vespucius or to his two expeditions of 1501 and 1503.

The learned historian Robertson observes: "It is remarkable that neither Gomara nor Oviedo, the most ancient Spanish historians of America, nor Herrera, consider Hojeda, or his companion Vespucius, as the first discoverers of the continent of America. They uniformly ascribe this honor to Columbus. Some have supposed that national resentment against Vespucius, for deserting the service of Spain, and entering into that of Portugal, may have prompted these writers to conceal the actions which he performed. But Martyr and Benzoni, both Italians, could not be warped by the same prejudice. Martyr was a contemporary author; he resided in the court of Spain, and had the best opportunity to be exactly informed with respect to all public transactions; and yet, neither in his Decades, the first gen-

[1] Histoire Philosophique et Politique des Établissemens et du Commerce des Européens dans les deux Indies Edition of 1786, Avignon. Vol. iv. p. 349.

eral history published of the New World, nor in his Epistles, which contain an account of all the remarkable events of his time, does he ascribe to Vespucius the honor of having first discovered the continent. Benzoni went as an adventurer to America in the year 1541, and resided there a considerable time. He appears to have been animated with a warm zeal for the honor of Italy, his native country, and yet does not mention the exploits and discoveries of Vespucius. Herrera, who compiled his general history of America from the most authentic records, not only follows those early writers, but accuses Vespucius of falsifying the dates of both the voyages which he made to the New World, and of confounding the one with the other, in order that he might arrogate to himself the glory of having discovered the continent."

Such are the opinions of one of the first among modern historians. And can it be supposed that a writer, as well informed as Robertson, could have been ignorant of the many works already written about Vespucius? No, they were all known to him; but able, learned, and impartial critic as he was, nothing except the truth found favor in his eyes. This accomplished Scotchman, remarkable for his great attainments, his love of method and indefatigable spirit of investigation, which was his most striking characteristic as an historian, refused to adopt the prevailing errors respecting Vespucius.[1]

[1] Robertson's History of America, Note xxii.

Castro (J. B.) a very learned Portuguese writer,[1] relying on the authority of Barros, Faria e Sousa,[2] Rocha Pitta,[3] and Brito Freire,[4] recounts the discovery of Brazil in 1500, without one word said of Vespucius.

Barbosa, the author of an excellent work called *Bibliotheca Lusitana* in his article upon Cabral, says, "this was the man who discovered America in 1500, and wrote an account of his voyage, which was published in the *Novus Orbis Regionum*, etc., of Grynæus, and in 1563 was printed in Italian at Venice."

Lacroix, in his *Géographie Moderne*, states that Brazil was discovered by Cabral in 1500, without mentioning Vespucius.

Camus, too, in his Memoir upon the voyages of Bry and Thévenot, published by order of the Institute of France in 1802, after having examined the different works upon the voyages of Vespucius, remarks upon the many absurdities which the narratives of this Florentine contain.

It was reserved for the writers of the 19th century to furnish us with a still more enlightened *critique* on this subject, and to some of them we now propose to refer.

The erudite professor Heeren, far from ascribing

[1] Mappa de Portugal.

[2] *Asia,* by Faria e Sousa. Vol. i. chap. 5, p. 1.

[3] America Portugueza.

[4] Nova Lusitania.

the discovery of Brazil to Vespucius, makes use of this expression: "And the coast of Brazil discovered and occupied (since 1500,) by Cabral."[1]

Pinkerton, although he says that a caprice of fortune gave the name of Vespucius to America, makes no allusion to his two voyages, of 1501 and 1503, to Brazil.

Mentelle,[2] instead of giving him the credit of having discovered this country, and citing his expeditions of 1501 and 1503, asserts: "*that Cabral, without a doubt, was the first European that ever saw the east coast of Brazil.*"

M. de Las Cases, in his *Atlas of Le Sage*, assigns to Columbus, when giving his chronological nomenclature of navigators, the first rank; and complains of the good fortune of Vespucius, who by a piece of injustice imposed his name on America.

"Thus, as says a certain historian," adds the author of the Atlas, "the first moment of the revelation of America's existence to the rest of the world, was stamped with iniquity,—fatal augury of what that unhappy country was about to become the scene."

In the *Dictionnaire Géographique* of Vosgien [Ladvocat], revised and enlarged by Malte-Brun, and in the edition of 1829, we find the following: "Chris-

[1] Historical Manual of the Political System of Europe, (English Transl., Oxford, 1834,) Vol. i. p. 43.

[2] Mentelle, *Géographie Universelle*, vol. xv. page 369.

topher Columbus discovered America in 1492, and gave it the name of West Indies: *that of America which has since prevailed is an injustice towards Columbus.*"

The authors of a Geographical Dictionary, published at Paris in 1823, and dedicated to M. de Humboldt, in their article on America, remark: "For the discovery of America we are indebted to Christopher Columbus, and even that of the Continent, in 1498, is attributed to him." But of Vespucius they say: "A Florentine, Americus Vespucius, accompanied Hojeda in this expedition, and on his return to Spain, he boasted of having been the first to discover the Continent of the New World." But they do not speak of the two voyages, said to have taken place in 1501 and 1503 by order of the king Emmanuel of Portugal. And in their article on Brazil is the following observation: "It was agreed to recognize Gonçalo Coelho as commander of the three vessels which left Lisbon in May, 1501, by the order of Emmanuel. A second squadron of six vessels, sent to sea a little time afterwards by the same sovereign, reconnoitered the Southern coast as far as the Cape *das Virgens*, and left a colony at Porto-Seguro."

The narratives of Vespucius have gained no credit with scarcely any English author in modern times, and especially since the commencement of the present century. The Encyclopedia Britannica begins its article on *America* in these words: "*America (from Americus Vespucius, falsely said to be the first discoverer of the Continent)*, &c. &c." and page 37, it thus continues: "*Columbus was the first European who set foot in the New World which he had discovered.*" Its authors, speaking of Brazil, relate the discovery of it made by Pedro Alvares Cabral, and refer to the annual expeditions sent by the Court of Portugal subsequently to that discovery; but not a solitary word escapes them relative to the pretended voyages of Vespucius in 1501 and 1503. Nor can any such be found in the *Edinburgh Gazetteer* or *Geographical Dictionary*, wherein Cabral alone is pronounced to have been the discoverer of Brazil.

Vespucius and his voyages of 1501 and 1503 are never once alluded to in the *History of Portugal*, a work originally written in English by a society of literary men, the materials for which were drawn from the most authentic sources, and in the illustrative notes to which, (amounting to 1553,) are cited a great number of authors, both foreign and Portuguese.[1] The only expeditions spoken of are those of Pedro Alvares Cabral, in 1500.

M. Bouvet de Cressé, in his *Maritime History of all Nations*,[2] says: "They with one accord have

[1] See the work cited, third Lisbon edit., (translation,) 1828. Vol. ii. pp. 231-235.

[2] Histoire de la Marine de tous les Peuples, etc. vol. i. Paris, 1824.

given to this new portion of the globe the name of America. *The impudent pretension of a lucky impostor has pilfered from the author of this discovery the glory that was his due. The name of America has supplanted that of Columbus.*")

These same sentiments in favor of Columbus are shared, at least in part, by Malte-Brun. The words of this learned geographer are:[1] "He (that is, Columbus) perceived that he had discovered a *new Continent, which ingratitude still calls America.*" And yet again,[2] without mentioning Vespucius: "Columbus and Vasco da Gama, by bursting through the imaginary confines which enchained the genius of the ancients, destroyed at one stroke the systems of Ptolemy and Strabo, and of the other geographers of antiquity."

We will not here analyze the opinion of this geographer, (elsewhere expressed,) respecting the fictitious first voyage of the Florentine to America, a year in advance of Columbus. It was grounded, without doubt, upon the narratives of Ramusio and especially of Canovai, the panegyrist of Vespucius; but the author of the continuation of his work seems not to have adopted it, seeing that in note 3d to page 518 of volume first, speaking of Vespucius, his words are: "*Excited, besides, by the success of Co-*

[1] Hist. de la Géographie, vol. i. page 617.

[2] Malte-Brun, vol. i. page 648. Paris, 1831.

*lumbus, he undertook his first voyage of discovery,"* &c., &c., &c., and in the first page of his second volume, he expresses himself yet more explicitly, as follows : "*We have again accompanied the immortal Columbus to this Continent, which ought by good rights to have been called after him.*"[1]

The learned Chevalier de Bossi, in his history of Christopher Columbus,[2] observes, "That the arrival of Columbus at Lisbon may be considered as the termination of his first voyage, the most important voyage of all, since it opened the New World to every age and to every nation. The very words of the illustrious Genoese himself furnish the best support to these facts. Happily there exists a letter written by his own hand, relative to the earliest American discoveries that had as yet been made, which was addressed to Raphaël Sanchez, the king of Spain's treasurer, and published at Lisbon in 1493. At Rome it was translated into Latin from the Spanish, and was twice printed in the same year, as the Chevalier Morelli supposes. Several biographers of Columbus mention this letter, and have even inserted it in their works. His own son, for example, among the rest has done this, and also a Genoese, by name Antonio Gallo, from whose pen there is a short trea-

[1] Précis de Géographie, vol. ii. Description of America.

[2] Histoire de Christophe Colomb, suivie de sa Correspondance, d'Éclaircissemens et de Pièces Curieuses et Inédites, traduite de l'Italien par C. M. Urano. Paris, 1824. See pages 155 and 156.

tise, entitled, *De navigatione Columbi per inaccessum antea Oceanum*, which is to be found in Muratori's collection. But this invaluable document, which for a long time has been regarded as the only thing written by Columbus and published during his life, the original of which, in Spanish, was printed, according to De Murr in the 15th century, has been several times given to the public, but so badly translated and so completely distorted, that one can with difficulty fancy he holds in his hands the authentic letter of Columbus. Fortunately, however, there still exists in the Brera library one copy of it, printed in 1493,[1] which has never elsewhere been met with either by myself or others, for the bibliographers themselves have never spoken of it. Fossi mentions another edition also of this letter, which dates from the 15th century, and which certainly must have fallen under the observation of very few persons; but, unless it be incomplete, it has nothing in common with that which is the subject of our consideration," &c.

What the Chevalier Bossi says in the passage just quoted adds weight to the authorities already cited by us, all of which prove that Columbus preceded Vespucius in the career of discovery. That too which follows (pages 170 and 179 inclusive,) respect-

[1] M. Ternaux, (Henri,) has a copy in his most valuable collection of Voyages, which he had the goodness to lend us.

ing the opinion of those who deny that Columbus was the first who ever saw the American Continent, is also so worthy of repetition that we think it ought to be transcribed in support of the sentiments contained in the previous chapters of this book. These are the words alluded to: [1] "Animated by a generous zeal, the author of the eulogy upon Columbus attempts to prove that it was that great man who first discovered the *terra firma* of America. He relies particularly upon Tiraboschi, and, besides the histories of Ferdinand, he cites Peter Martyr d'Anghiera, and a narrative printed in 1508 at Milan. He might have appealed to many other works, but *his special object is to assure to Columbus the glory of that discovery which was claimed for Americus Vespucius.* He appears to be contradicted by the Spanish authors, who date the voyage of the Tuscan navigator to the West Indies, not in 1497, which would place it a year in advance of Columbus's third voyage, but in 1499. It is possible that, either through error, or for the sake of assuming to himself the honor of the discovery, Vespucius may have antedated his letters upon this epoch by two years, for no other testimony has presented itself in his favor; and the rather that in 1496 Columbus directed his steps towards Spain, and never left that country till 1498; which proves that he was at the

[1] Ibid. p. 170.

Spanish court in 1497. At that epoch, already had been issued, without scruple and to his detriment, many licenses to go in quest of new discoveries. Of these Columbus with great reason complained, and the court, which still had an interest in handling him tenderly, consequently revoked them. It must be supposed, then, that in this interval Vespucius set sail with Hojeda, the bitter enemy of Columbus, who at the moment was in the full enjoyment of court favor. . . . . . . .

"Hojeda took his departure with Vespucius a year subsequently to the third voyage of Columbus, and when the latter was beginning to fall into disgrace at court. . . . . . In fact, Hojeda did not reach Saint Domingo till 1499, a long time after the arrival of Columbus, who had already coasted the New Continent. What could they have been about these two years, Hojeda and Vespucius, who, according to the latter's story, did not even land upon those shores, which they pretend, besides, were first seen by them? How can we account for the silence of Columbus himself in the matter, — of him who noted every thing in his letters, and who was incapable of stifling his complaints when he thought there was cause for them? How, too, is it to be explained that contemporary historians say no more on this point than he?" *And notwithstanding all this*, cries the author of the eulogy of Columbus, in his anguish, *Americus Vespucius enjoyed the unmerited glory of giving his name to this part of the world, and an indifferent posterity has sanctioned a decision, which injustice pronounced against Christopher, and which the lapse of ages has henceforth forever rendered irreparable.*

"But," continues the Chevalier Bossi, "neither Tiraboschi nor the author of the eulogy employed themselves in refuting those writers who, for the purpose of assuring the Florentine navigator's glory, pretend that Christopher never left the neighborhood of Saint Domingo, Jamaica, Cuba, and the other islands of the Mexican archipelago. However, without stopping now to examine the accounts, contained in several histories, of this voyage of Columbus along the coasts of the main land, it seems to us that the letter of the Genoese navigator by itself, the same which Morelli first published, establishes the fact beyond a doubt."

The author then analyzes the letter in question, and indicates an important passage, contrasting it with what Hornius says in his *Origines Americanæ*, and afterwards adds the following observations upon Vespucius: — "A number of writers relate that Americus, before undertaking his voyage to the New World, visited England and Ireland, and that, on quitting these countries, he penetrated so far into the North Sea that he was compelled by the ice to effect a hasty retreat.[1] But all these stories have no other

[1] Perhaps he was confounded with Cortereal.

foundation than the narrative of Girolamo Bartolommei, who composed a poem in the sixteenth century, called *America*, in which, by a poetic fiction, he conducts Vespucius to the court of the King of Ethiopia, and there makes him give an account of his imaginary voyages in the northern seas! . . . . .

"The partisans of Vespucius," the chevalier adds, "even deny that Columbus ever left the islands he discovered in order to approach the main land; but they offer no proof in support of their denial, except the testimony of Francesco Giuntini, who flourished about one hundred years later; while in favor of Columbus is invoked the evidence of authors contemporary with Peter Martyr d'Anghiera, (by whom the country of Paria was pointed out as the American Continent,) and of others that lived at the same time with him who wrote the *Narrative of Voyages*, which was printed at the commencement of the sixteenth century at Venice and at Milan.

"Was Vespucius the chief of the expedition sent to America, or did he embark as a simple passenger?" asks Bossi. "Here is another subject of doubt which still requires investigation. All the Spanish writers who describe the voyage in which Vespucius figured, assert that it did not take place till 1499, and that the Archbishop of Badajoz, the enemy of Columbus, sent orders, signed by himself alone, to Alonso de Hojeda, directing him to proceed to the New World, and there to attempt new discoveries, which he hoped might obscure the glory of Columbus, who happened to be at Saint Domingo at the moment, and who must have been ignorant of the treachery practised against him in Spain.

"Hojeda had for his pilot Juan de la Cosa, a native of Biscay, and, according to the same writers, Americus Vespucius went as a simple passenger,[1] and, in quality of merchant, had nothing but a pecuniary interest in the armament. Indeed, the latter, whenever he speaks, always makes use of the plural number, expressing himself thus, for example: *We went, we debarked, &c. &c.*,[2] and he does not profess to have formed part of the royal Spanish commission except in one solitary letter, addressed to Lorenzo de' Medici. Here, then, we probably have the motives which prevented Peter Martyr d'Anghiera from ever classing Vespucius among the discoverers of the New World, while at the same time he gave him due praise for his knowledge of geography and astronomy.[3]

"In the account of his second voyage," concludes the author we have been quoting, "if perchance he ever made one before it, Vespucius suffers to appear a certain feeling of jealousy against the individual who had first visited the new hemisphere. The voyages made by this Florentine at a later period,

[1] See our opinion in Chap. i. Letter to M. de Navarrete, p. 229 of the *Bulletin de la Société Géographique.*

[2] Ibid. [3] Ibid.

were undertaken by order of the court of Portugal, and it was then that he attributed to himself the honor of having discovered Brazil, an honor which the Spaniards denied him, and which the Portuguese ascribed to one of their own countrymen, Pedro Alvares Cabral, in 1500."

## CHAPTER III.

SINCE the appearance of the works of the writers and geographers above cited, M. de Navarrete has published the third volume of his *Coleccion de los Viages y Descubrimientos que hicieron por mar los Españoles* &c., &c., in which he treats of Vespucius more in detail, examines more accurately the several accounts of his voyages, critically contrasts the different editions of those productions which speak of this Florentine, and in this manner puts us in possession of researches full of interest, and meriting the utmost attention from every critic.[1] We refer the reader to this Spanish author's own words, but as his third volume has not yet been translated,[2] we think it should be remarked that M. de Navarrete clearly demonstrates that Bandini and Canovai, the panegyrists of Vespucius, were not sufficiently acquainted with the Lorraine edition of the *Cosmographiæ Introductio*, &c., &c., which contains the voyages of this Florentine, and he shows that Vespucius himself, in certain portions of the narrative of his expedition in 1497, *copied the Memoir of Columbus.*

[1] Among others, see those in the note, pp. 242, 243.

[2] The two first volumes were translated by Messrs. de la Roquette and de Verneuil.

M. de Navarrete assures us, at page 243, that according to Vespucius's history of his second voyage, the distance of the territory indicated by him, corresponds to 666 maritime leagues and two thirds of a league, in a south-west course, which would have placed him and his vessels upon the American Continent, 165 leagues from the sea, and in the northern part of Brazil! and moreover, that the same route in latitude five degrees south would have brought him nearly fifty-eight leagues into the interior. Hence we see, he exclaims, how many errors and false statements are to be found in these narratives.

In the 2d note to page 265 it is proved that the south-west course described by Vespucius in his account, and the distance he gives of 700 leagues, (933 maritime leagues and a third,) would have put the travellers upon the South American Continent, in south latitude nineteen degrees and fifteen minutes, 390 *leagues in the interior of the country, and consequently equally distant from the coast where they should have been at anchor.*

On the subject of Vespucius's self-contradictions, our author asks: "*How is it possible to conceive that the territory in question was taken possession of in the name of the king of Castile, if the voyage had been made by order of the king of Portugal?* And in the second note to page 274, he remarks upon the astronomical observations of Vespucius, what is not less important, "that it is impossible to understand what is meant by his diameters and semi-diameters, which he talks of for the second time, and for this reason, that the prodigious distance, according to Lalande, which the stars are from us, must prevent the slightest sensation of wonder at the extreme smallness of their apparent diameter, and that we are unable to compute their absolute size and true diameter. And if so distinguished an astronomer as Lalande,"[1] continues M. de Navarrete, "has established this fact in our day, how is it possible that, at the end of the 15th and beginning of the 16th centuries, astral diameters and semi-diameters could have been measured with such rude instruments as were used by our navigators of that epoch? And then, too, the vessel Vespucius speaks of in the text of his letter he says was only a small bark, with a crew of four or five persons,[2] in which it is hardly possible to believe that he could have made the preceding passage of 300 leagues to Bahia, or the later one of 260, to the port where he pretends a chateau was constructed, and where his vessel remained. Added to which, his vessel remaining there, how could he have returned to Lisbon?"

There are yet other critical remarks, of great interest, to be found in M. de Navarrete's *Noticias exactas de Américo Vespucio*, from the 315th to the

[1] Astronomie, Liv. xvi. No. 2784.

[2] See page 287, note 2, vol. iii.

334th page; and in the course of his examination our author has adopted the hypothesis first published by us, in July, 1826, respecting the two expeditions of 1501 and 1503, in saying, "that Vespucius might have made the voyages, as a personage entirely unknown, in the ships to Brazil; just as he did in the first enterprize of Hojeda;" and, with us, he observes, that, even in accordance with the statements of Vespucius himself, it is probable that that navigator did sail along the coast of Brazil, and saw how Cape Saint Augustine was situated, yet only as a subaltern on board of some Portuguese vessel, which left the port of Lisbon between 1501 and 1504, but that, Brazil having been reconnoitred in January of 1500, by Pedro Alvares Cabral, Pinzon, Lepe and others, and Vasco da Gama having already finished his voyage the 10th of July, 1499, and returned to Portugal, after his grand discoveries in the East, it consequently follows that the Florentine was not the discoverer of those seas and countries.

The learned Spanish academician afterwards contests, with an enlightened criticism, the pretensions of Bandini and Canovai, the two panegyrists of Vespucius, in such a manner that it would be useless for us here to point out their errors and evident contradictions. Nevertheless we will make a few observations which we have not found either in the investigations of M. de Navarrete or of other writers and geographers.

Besides the confusion and incoherence found in the narratives of Vespucius's voyages, as already indicated by the authors above cited, facts of the like nature, and not less important in our opinion, occur in his *Dedication* to René, Duke of Lorraine, (who styled himself king of Sicily and Jerusalem,) which is contained in the *Cosmographiæ Introductio, insuper quatuor Americi Vespucii Navigationes*, printed at Saint Diey, in Lorraine, in 1507, wherein the name of *America* for the first time appears.

Now this René of Anjou, who called himself king, died at Aix in 1480,[1] and consequently Vespucius could not have written, or addressed his narrations to him four and twenty years after his decease. Neither could any relations have existed between the Duke and the Florentine respecting the voyages of the latter, nor could one have been the patron of the other, before a single expedition was undertaken. And it so happens that Duke René the 1st, the great protector of Huber, Van-Eyck, Botinelli, Perugino, Philelphus, Maggio, Marcel, Martial d'Auvergne, and of other celebrated men, died ten years before the arrival of Vespucius in Spain ; and it was not till 1499, or nineteen years after the decease of that prince, that the first voyage of this navigator, mentioned by several authors and geographers, took place.

[1] Bodin, Recherches Historiques sur l'Anjou, vol. i. page 508; Koch, vol. iii. tabl. 133; Biographie Universelle, vol. xxxvii.

It is impossible, too, that Vespucius could have been brought up with the prince, as he asserts he was in the same dedication of the work quoted,[1] for an examination of dates and facts shows most conclusively that the Duke of Lorraine spoken of was not René the 1st.

Vespucius was born at Florence, the 9th of March, 1451, and Duke René the 1st, king of Sicily and Jerusalem, at the Chateau of Angers, the 16th of January, 1409.[2] So that the latter was forty-two years of age at the birth of the former, and of course there could have been between them no youthful intimacy, nor could they have studied together the rudiments of grammar at Florence. The prince received his early education under the eyes of his mother at *Angers*, and at the court of France, while Vespucius was brought up in Italy.

The first connection that this duke of Lorraine ever had with Italy dates only from the year 1434, when he sent there, with the title of lieutenant, the queen Isabella, his wife, that she might retain the

1 . . . . . . Ubi recordabitur quod *olim mutuam habuerimus amicitiam, tempore juventutis nostræ, cum grammaticæ rudimenta imbibentes sub probata vita et doctrina venerabilis fratris de S. Marco, Frat. Georgii Antonii Vespucii, avunculi mei, pariter militaremus*, etc.

2 Date from the Biographie Universelle. Bodin, Recherches Historiques sur l'Anjou, vol. i. page 502, in which it is said that this prince was born in 1408. The same date, too, is found in the History of René, by Villeneuve, vol. i., while other writers carry back the date of his birth to 1407 — a year earlier, thus ascribing to him forty-four years of age when Vespucius was born.

Pope and the duke of Milan in his interests, reanimate there the zeal of the Angers party, and foil the intrigues of the king of Aragon. He did not visit Genoa and Naples till 1438, and returned to France by way of Marseilles at the end of 1442, and before Vespucius was born.[1] When he went to Italy a second time, where he did not stay long, he was forty-six years of age and Vespucius only two.

If the same difficulties do not present themselves, on the supposition that the Duke René of Lorraine, spoken of in Vespucius's dedication, and entitled king of Sicily and Jerusalem, was René the Second, still we remark that there are yet others which we will indicate.

Although this second duke of Lorraine, who, according to some modern authorities,[2] also assumed the title of king of Sicily and Jerusalem, was contemporary with Vespucius, the history of his life alone suffices to show that he had no youthful relations with the Florentine. Not one of the many writers of Lorraine says that he ever was in Italy previously to his journey to Venice in 1480, where he negotiated a treaty with that republic, nor does any one of them assert that he was educated at Florence. And, moreover, as he was twenty-nine years of age on

[1] See the Histories of Lorraine.

[2] We have met with no contemporary document which proves that this duke took this title, nor is one to be found among the authorities cited by the learned D. Calmet, in his *Histoire Ecclésiastique et Civile de la Lorraine*.

going to Italy for the first time, it is not likely that he then took to the study of grammar! — he who was employed in negotiating treaties, and received the appointment of lieutenant-general to the armies of the republic. These are facts likewise anterior to that epoch (1480), which render still more obvious the improbability of what Vespucius's dedication contains.

We find that René II. resided at Joinville till 1473, that is, till his twenty-first year, at which time one of the Lorraine historians tells us,[1] that scarcely was duke Nicolas dead, when a German captain arrived at Joinville, under the pretext of felicitating the young Count of Vaudémont, but in reality for the purpose of getting René out of the hands of his mother, in which he succeeded; and that it was in consequence of this high-handed offence that the Duke of Burgundy began to put in execution the plan he had formed for invading the territory of Lorraine, which Louis II. regarded with such horror, that he caused the nephew of the emperor to be arrested at Paris by way of reprisal, and *obliged the duke to restore René to Yolande.*

Besides, in addition to the fact that not an individual historian utters a word about René II. having been educated at Florence, in company with Vespucius and under the direction of the navigator's uncle, there is another yet more important, which is, that Bandini himself, the principal panegyrist of

[1] Bexon, p. 156.

Americus, quotes at page 25th of his second chapter, a passage from Giuliano Ricci, the celebrated antiquary, in which the scholars of Antonio Vespucius are mentioned by name, as follows: "Antonio Vespucius gave lessons in grammar to young persons of the nobility, and among his disciples were Piero di Messer Tomaso Soderini and Americus Vespucius."

Now if René II., a prince, had been of this number, and too the companion of Americus, would the antiquarian Ricci and the panegyrist Bandini been likely to have forgotten so interesting a circumstance, especially the latter, who had made such minute inquiries, and enters into such particular details respecting the education and genealogy of his hero? But even he seems not to have been insensible to the incongruity of this dedication, as he evidently shunned an examination which might have resulted disastrously for the memory of his idol, and for the pretended authenticity of documents published by him, or by the theoretical speculators upon that epoch, or by his friends, at the commencement of the sixteenth century, a century so rife with literary forgers of every description.

Next we propose to enter upon some other questions, suggested by the dates of these letters of Vespucius, which are addressed now to Lorenzo de' Medici, now to Lorenzo Piero de' Medici, and then again to Lorenzo di Pier Francesco de' Medici of

Florence.[1] They are dated the 18th of July, 1500, May 1501, and, according to others, 1504.

If this Lorenzo Piero de' Medici was, as would appear from the earliest editions, that Lorenzo called the *Magnificent*, who had assumed the name of his father, Piero I., this prince, it is to be remarked, died in 1442.[2] How then could have Vespucius addressed to him letters upon his pretended voyages when he was no longer in existence? And if this critically well-founded observation be not sufficient to prove beyond dispute what confusion, whether accidental or designed, whether caused by himself or others, is found in the accounts of Vespucius's voyages at this epoch, the silence of Valori, Fabronio,[3] and Roscoe, three such conscientious historians of the two Lorenzos de' Medici, would furnish us with a serious motive for being upon our guard. They, indeed, say not a word of any connection whatever having existed between these princes and Vespucius, nor do they speak of any letter from this Florentine upon a subject so all-important as the discovery of a New World! The same silence likewise prevails in the *Diario de successi importanti seguite*, etc., from 1498 to 1512, a contemporary work, published at Florence in 1568, by Biagio Buonacorsi, which comprehends the period when the

1 See the most ancient editions. 2 See the biographers.

3 This writer speaks of a certain Guido Antonio Vespucius, but says nothing of Americus.

voyages of Vespucius were made and his letters were written. And the silence of this author is the more significant, not merely because he wrote about the remarkable things that happened in Italy and at Florence, addressing himself to natives of that city, celebrated at the epoch when Vespucius and his partisans propagated their first accounts of the fabulous discoveries, contained in his letters to Soderini and the Medici, which treated of an event of such vast importance that all Europe knew, or ought to have known of it, but also because the king Emmanuel communicated every new discovery to the court of Rome, through the embassy of Tristam da Cunha, at the end of the fifteenth century, as likewise to the Venetian government; and a contemporary Florentine author, therefore, could not but have been certain as to these said letters, whether or not they were addressed to Soderini and Lorenzo de' Medici.

But those who support the pretensions of Vespucius will perhaps say that his letters were written, not to Lorenzo de' Medici, called *the Magnificent*, but to Lorenzo II. We have already shown that in the first editions it is the name of Lorenzo Piero which is found, and that consequently it was Lorenzo, surnamed the Magnificent, to whom these epistles were addressed. But, supposing that it was not he, if it be said that it was Lorenzo II. the answer then is, that the latter prince, having been born the

13th of September, 1492, could not have attained his eighth year when Vespucius's first letter was written, and we would ask, if it is probable that a report of voyages and discoveries would have been made to a child?

Bandini saw very plainly what a stretch of credulity was here required, and how much the reputation of his hero would suffer from an analysis like ours; he sought therefore to give to this letter an air of genuineness, by saying that perhaps this Lorenzo de' Medici was a certain *Lorenzo di Pier Francesco.* But it will be evident that this conjecture not only shakes the authenticity of the document itself, but that it is in direct opposition to a part of his own text, where he says: "*It cannot be denied that it* [the letter] *is addressed to a Lorenzo, whilst in the body of the same he gives him the title of Magnificent.*"

Besides that this conjecture of Bandini's[1] is *contra producentem*, it is not supported, nor do we believe it can be supported by the rules of correct criticism.

We have just seen, by the preceding simple analysis merely of the personages to whom Vespucius's letters were addressed, how much difficulty,

[1] The opinion of Robertson on Bandini is in these words: "In 1745, the Abbé Bandini published at Florence a life of Vespucius in 4to." "This work, which has no merit, is written with as little judgment as truth. The author supports the pretensions of his countryman to the discovery of the New World, with all the zeal which a national prejudice inspires, but he brings no proof to sustain them."

See History of America, by Robertson, published at Paris in 1827, with notes drawn from the works of M. de Humboldt.

inconsistency, and confusion exist respecting the authenticity of these documents. To this we will add, that it is impossible for us to understand how, at the epoch spoken of, — the time of king Emmanuel, — Vespucius, who at one moment was in the service of Spain, the next in that of Portugal, and then again in that of Spain, (that is, if his story and that of certain authors and geographers be true,) how he dared to sustain a correspondence with any of the Medici, and nearly at the same time with Soderini, when the former were declared rebels to the republic of Florence, their native country, and the latter was detested and prosecuted by the court of Rome and Pope Julius II., who protected the Medici, and exercised a powerful influence both in Portugal and Spain. Nor can we conceive how he could allow himself, amid the ideas prevailing at his time and under such influences as then existed, to write to parties so opposed in character to each other as were the Medici and Soderini. For, in addressing himself to one of the Medicean family, he compromised himself with the government of his own country, and in corresponding with Soderini he could not fail to expose himself to the anger of the court of Rome, and to excite the suspicions of those of Spain and Portugal. And equally astonishing is it, that, when the works of three celebrated travellers, foreigners by birth, were printed in Portuguese at Lisbon in 1502, those containing the discoveries of Vespucius, which he pretended to have made before that date, and by the orders of the king himself, were not at the same time published at Lisbon, but were given to the public in Lorraine, whither their author went for that express purpose.[1] The names of the three travellers alluded to were, Marco Polo, Nicolo, a Venetian, whom Ortelius calls Nicolo di Conti, and a certain Girolamo da Santo Stefano, a Genoese, who in 1499 had written from Tripoli to one of his friends in Germany an account of his voyages.

Some persons would fain insist, according to what we have set forth, that a document cannot be condemned as false by negative arguments, or by the silence of one or several authors; but the *savans* who composed the *Nouveau Traité de Diplomatique*, and who are an authority in the matter, remark with justice: *unless it was impossible that they* (the authors) *should not have spoken of it, if it had been true.* And, in our opinion, it is precisely in this light in the case before us, that we should regard the silence of Barros, Goes, Osorio, Buonacorsi, and Valori, authors living at the time of the event in question, and when Vespucius set up his pretensions. In the same sense also ought to be taken the silence of the contemporary documents of the general archives of Portugal, that of more than two hundred Portuguese manuscripts in the royal library at Paris, and above all that of No. 10,023, entitled, *Journal of the*

[1] The letter of Columbus was also published at Lisbon, in 1493.

*Voyages of the Portuguese, from* 1497 *to* 1682. Equally conclusive, too, is the silence of 703 volumes of a collection of Italian manuscripts in the same library, of which M. Marsand has lately published a catalogue, and in which the name of Vespucius is not so much as mentioned. Nor is it to be found in the catalogues of several thousands of manuscripts contained in 432 libraries, catalogues of which by M. Haenel, have been published.[1]

Critics, severe and conscientious, would, without doubt, characterize as forgeries the documents published about Vespucius at the commencement of the sixteenth century, after having followed us in our

[1] Nicolao d'Oliveira, a Portuguese author at the end of the sixteenth century, who wrote a history of Brazil, which, according to Barbosa, in his Portuguese Library, remained unpublished, preserved the same silence as to Vespucius.

In a work, published in Latin at Leyden, in 1641, by the Elzevirs, and entitled, Portugalia, sive De Regis Portugaliæ Regnis et Opibus Commentarius, we find, at page 191, a passage by the Portuguese author, which is in opposition to the pretension of Vespucius.

And here is the observation of the commentator upon the authority of the Portuguese author: "*It was, according to Nicolao d'Oliveira, in Southern America that the king of Portugal possessed the territory of Brazil, which was formerly called the province of Santa Cruz by the Portuguese*, who first discovered and explored it," &c.

Morisot, in his *Orbis Maritimus*, cites the same Portuguese author and pronounces Columbus to have been the first discoverer of America. . . . . . . . . . . . .

"*Since these islands, a later age discovered a fourth part of the world, called America from Americus Vespucius, who, however, was not the first navigator there, but Columbus, in whose steps he followed*," &c.

Nevertheless, Morisot does not mention the two fictitious voyages of 1501 and 1503.

examination of them; for they bear upon their very face every sign of being such, according to the established usages of diplomatic criticism. And this appears so, because it is the peculiar quality of a forgery to run counter to the supposed necessary accordance which should exist between a document and the age in which it was written; because counterfeit documents involve in contradiction *both the subjects and the authors of them;*[1] *because one solitary, but important mistake, which, morally speaking, could never have found its way into a genuine document, destroys the authenticity of the piece of which it forms a part;*[2] because *capital errors in history and chronology*, such as we have brought to light in this work, *produce the firmest conviction of the crime of falsification;*[3] and lastly, because, according to another rule of diplomatic criticism, *one single fact* which cannot be made to correspond with such and such personages and circumstances, forming the subject matter of a document, *is quite sufficient to condemn that document as a forgery.*[4] Now, in the letters of Vespucius, under our present consideration, it is not *one isolated fact*, but *many facts*, which, beyond a doubt, cannot be made to correspond with the persons and circumstances he writes about. The ancient partisans of these errors might have

[1] Nouveau Traité de Diplomatique, vol. vi. p. 289.

[2] Ibid.

[3] Work already cited.

[4] Ibid. p. 311.

argued, that at the time of Vespucius they were spread abroad with the impress of truth upon them; but, to say nothing of the impress of truth in the opinion of one century becoming the impress of falsehood in that of another,[1] we meet with an infinite quantity of printed documents, once bearing the character of authenticity, which are now admitted to be spurious. It will be sufficient to advert, as examples, to the seventeen books published at the end of the fifteenth century, (the epoch when Vespucius flourished,) by Annius of Viterbo, and to those of Bivar, published under the name of Flavius Dexter, documentary impostures fabricated by *La Higuera*. Nevertheless, these impostures were regarded for a time as genuine, and later historians have been duped by them.

The history of forgers of all sorts of memorials would form by itself an immense collection of volumes, and especially the history of those belonging to the fifteenth and sixteenth centuries, in which would appear a number of *savans* that became their victims.

A very learned German (Schlegel)[2] remarks, "that the book of the fables of Reinecke Fuchs can be mentioned as an instance of what the world was in the fourteenth and fifteenth centuries.[3] This

[1] Nouveau Traité de Diplomatique, vol. vi.
[2] History of Literature, vol. i. p. 401.
[3] The epoch of the birth of Vespucius.

work," says he, "*shows how among chevaliers and citizens, kings and people, those who were the most honest were often the most cheated.*" . . . . .

Have there not been, too, at no great distance from our own times, certain facts which support what we say? Everybody has heard of the Prince of Orange's medal, on which was inscribed: *Portus gratiæ exustus et eversus bombardis Anglo-Batavii, MDCXCIII.* (The port of Hâvre burnt and destroyed by the Anglo-Dutch bombardment in 1693.) And yet if the bombardment of Hâvre be a true fact, the ruin of Hâvre is a false one. So if the discovery of the New World is a true fact, the priority of this discovery by Vespucius, at the expense of Columbus, Cabral, and Coelho, is likewise a false one. But, admitting that the injustice committed against these three be irremediable, (for errors allowed and consecrated by the lapse of ages often triumph over science,) still *against Truth there is no prescription, and however we may have strayed from it, there is always time to return, since by the aid of time faults, errors, and forgeries may be detected, which at first had eluded discovery.*[1]

And this injustice is the more offensive, according to the opinion of an illustrious *savant*, M. de Humboldt, because, as he says, "*It was an obscure man who invented the name of America, and who proposed it in his work* (above cited) *called: Cosmographiæ*

[4] Nouveau Traité de Diplomatique, by the Benedictines.

*Introductio, insuper quatuor Americi Vespucii Navigationes*,[1] which name Apian, Vadianus, and Camers have since widely spread through Strasburg, Friburg, and Vienna, while the prodigious celebrity of the little book of Apian *has propagated the evil* by innumerable editions in Holland and elsewhere."

We have above shown not only in what way should be characterized this first work of 1507, published in Lorraine, in which for the first time the name of America is found under the title *Cosmographiæ Introductio*, &c. a work that has been the origin of so much injustice, mistake, and disorder, but also what name ought to be bestowed on Vespucius's letters to Lorenzo de' Medici and Soderini, published at Paris in 1516, and at Milan in 1519, which were a prolific source of error and confusion before Apian's production made its appearance. And in our opinion, a critical examination, whose object is to repair injustice and establish facts, must always not only be worthy of science, but likewise an additional homage to truth itself.

[1] Chronology of the most ancient Maps of America. Note published in the Bulletin of the Geographical Society, December, 1841. M. de Humboldt observes, that the map of Apian (1520) "in imposing the name of America on the Southern Continent, says that it was discovered in 1497 by Columbus, (this is the year precisely of Vespucius's pretended discovery, joined to the name of Columbus,) whilst that in the cosmographical work of Peter Apian, carefully corrected by Gemma Frisio, (Antwerp, 1529,) we read as follows: '*The fourth portion of the world derived its name from Americus Vespucius, the discoverer of the same. It was discovered in the year* 1497."

## CHAPTER IV.

WHENEVER an interval of several ages separates us from an event which was doubtful at the time it happened, the greatest difficulty is encountered in attempting to establish and elucidate it. Such is our position relative to the problematical expeditions of Americus Vespucius. And the difficulty is increased in our day by the immense study required in the examination of a host of books and documents, which have been published since the beginning of the sixteenth century, an epoch when error and disorder brought forth so many false judgments upon the question we have in hand. The manifest contradictions, too, of a great number of writers, both as to dates and facts, adds still more to our embarrassment.

In this labyrinth, it struck us that our purpose would not be answered by simply confining ourselves to an analysis of the narrations imputed to Vespucius, and contrasting them with accounts either of those navigators who preceded him, or who were prosecuting discoveries at the moment when his letters were given to the world. We therefore felt ourselves compelled to subject this point in geographical history to a clear and accurate examination, either by resting for support on a great amount of testimony which has been neglected by critics that have gone before us, or by submitting to a fresh scrutiny the works which have been already quoted. It was in consequence of these considerations that we have entered upon this question in a manner altogether peculiar, and, if we may be permitted to say so, equally new. The nature of our public duties has obliged us since 1826 to interrupt these investigations; and then, too, a number of literary undertakings, besides the scarceness of certain books and the time required to find and study them, have forced us to make our investigation piecemeal, as it were, and thus to present the result of our researches somewhat in detached portions, and, it may be, without method. So that the notes hitherto published by us in the Bulletin of the Geographical Society, and this continuation to them, are to be considered only as mere essays preparatory to a future work of more methodical construction.

Painful as it may be to us to fatigue the reader with a long series of extracts and increased quotations, we will take the liberty of remarking, that, in this important inquiry, these are so many pieces, hitherto discussed in a sense entirely opposed to our own, but indispensably necessary for the enlightenment of those on whose judgments rests a final decision.

We have shown that the famous *Introduction to*

*Cosmography*, printed at Saint Diey, in Lorraine, in 1507, was the principal source of error, together with the numerous collections of letters of Vespucius published at the commencement of the sixteenth century.[1] To these we will add yet another production of the same year, the mendacious title of which served to increase still further the existing confusion. It is the collection of Montalboddo Francanzano, a very rare book, printed at Vicenza in 1507, and fraudulently entitled, *Paesi novamente retrovati et Novo Mondo da Alberico Vesputio, Fiorentino, intitulato.* It was translated into French, and printed in that language, at Paris, in 1513,[2] by Philippe Le Noir, with the following title, far surpassing the original in extravagance, *Le Nouveau Monde et Nauigations faictes par Emeric de Vespuce, Florentin, des pays et isles nouuellement trouvéz, auparauãt ĩcongneuz, tant en l'Etiope q' Arrabie, Calichut et aultres plusieurs régions estranges. Translaté de ytalien en langue françoyse, par Mathurin de Redouer.* Two other editions of this translation were printed at Paris, without any indication of date, by

[1] This publication was preceded by that of the *Mundus Novus, magister Johannes Otmar Vindelice impressit Auguste, anno* 1504; by that entitled, *De ora Antarctica, per regem Portugalliæ pridem inventa. Impressum Argentine per Mathiam Hupfuff*, 1505; and by that entitled, *Von den nuwen insulen und landen so ietzt kürtzlichen erfunden synt durch den künig von Portugal*, Strasburg, 1506.

[2] The "Art de verifier les Dates," fixes this to be the date. See vol. xii. third part, p. 110.

Jehan Janot, and by Jean Trepperel. Of these, we have seen the latter at the Royal Library, and have already quoted it. Judging from the date of the *privilege*, it seems to have been printed in 1516. We have found, too, another edition in the splendid collection of Mr. Henry Ternaux.[1]

The indication, according to the original edition, of subjects contained in this work, is as follows: —

1. *A Book of the first Voyage by Sea to the Land of the Negroes, in Lower Ethiopia, by command of the most illustrious Seignior, the Infant Don Henry, brother of Don Edward, King of Portugal.*

2. *The second Book of the Navigation from Lisbon to Calicut, in Italian, from the Portuguese Language.* We will observe, that in this book is found *the account of the voyage of Pedro Alvares Cabral, and of the discovery which he made of the land of Santa Cruz* (Brazil.)

3. *The third Book of the Navigation from Lisbon to Calicut, in the Italian, from the Portuguese Language.* At the end of it we read, *And now commences the navigation of the islands and countries of the King of Castile, lately discovered.* This book begins by a narrative of the expedition of Columbus.

[1] The edition in M. Ternaux's possession was published at Paris, by Gaillot-du-Pré. The copy in the Royal Library comes from that of Falconet. Respecting these collections, see Brunet, catalogue de la Vallière; Meusel, Biblioth. Hist. vol. iii. p. 265; Memoir of Sebastian Cabot, 1831, p. 241.

"*Christopher Columbus,*" it says, "*a Genoese, was a man of lofty and noble stature, of a reddish complexion, broad face, and great genius.*"

It is not till these voyages and narratives are all finished, that we find these words, in the fifth book of this collection: "*The New World, translated from the Spanish Language into the Roman Idiom, (book fifth.) From Alberic Vespucius to Lorenzo Piero de' Medici, greeting.*" This is the letter to Lorenzo Piero de' Medici. But in the same book is found the letter of the envoy of the Venetian Republic, who resided at Lisbon,[1] that of the ambassador of the same republic, Pascoaligo,[2] and other letters and narratives, which, so far from favoring the pretensions of Vespucius, add still further to the doubt and uncertainty that exist as to the reality of his voyages. One of these letters, dated 1502, and posterior to the month of March, appears to have been written by some of those Italian merchants who were settled in Portugal, to their correspondents at Florence or Venice. In it they give a long and detailed account of the expeditions of Cabral to Calicut, and of the productions of India and Western Africa; they speak of particular concessions granted by the king, at the rate of thirty-seven per cent.; they make a display of their erudition, and talk of

[1] Before cited. [2] Cited before.

Solomon and of the Queen of Sheba, as touching Sophala,[1] and cite Pliny when discoursing of Taprobane[2]; they manifest the influence which biblical instruction and a perusal of the old classics had had upon the spirit of discovery; but not a word do they say of Vespucius, or of his pretended voyage of the preceding year. Another of these letters is dated at Lisbon, the sixteenth of September of the same year, (1502,) and is written by Francesco di Santa Cremona to Pascoaligo, the Venetian Ambassador, who happened at that moment to be in Spain. In it we find details the most minute, respecting the voyages then in course of execution, and even upon the vessels which were being built in the ports of Portugal for expeditions of the like nature; but, notwithstanding the date of September, 1502, no mention whatever is made of Vespucius.

The striking difference which exists, as has already been proved, between the actual contents of the collection spoken of and the fraudulent announcement on the titlepage, suffices to demonstrate what serious errors were spread abroad by such publications, at an epoch when enthusiasm for voyages and discoveries fascinated entire Europe almost, and caused to be received with rabid credulity the pompous enunciations of a mendacious title.

[1] Sofala, perhaps the Ophir of Solomon.
[2] Ceylon.

This collection was unknown to Camus;[1] for he acknowledges that what he says of it was taken from Tiraboschi;[2] and not having been able to examine it himself, he thought that for the most part it contained only the narrative of Vespucius. Whereas, quite the contrary is the fact, as we have just seen. Camus cites a pamphlet of six sheets, (said by Maittaire and Panzer to be extremely rare,) which has for its title, *Albericus Vespucius Laurentio Petri Francisci de Medicis salutem plurimam dicit;* beneath which is seen the name of Jehan Lambert, a printer who exercised his art at Paris from 1493 to 1514. It contains an account of the voyage of 1501, in Latin; and he adds, that some persons have decided the date of this edition to be of the same year. Now, this pamphlet, which is in the Royal Library, we have examined; and not only must we withhold from it the date supposed, but we are constrained to believe that neither Camus nor those who admitted its genuineness ever reflected on the impossibility of reconciling with it the date of the pretended voyage. How, indeed, could it have been possible to print at Paris in 1501, the narrative of an enterprise, which Vespucius says was undertaken by him on quitting Lisbon, the same year, in the month of May, and which must have

[1] Mémoires sur les grands Voyages.

[2] Tiraboschi, vol. vii. part i. p. 213.

lasted, according to one of these letters, sixteen months, and according to another, perhaps twenty?[1] Consequently, the said narrative could not have been printed, nor even written, the fourth of September of that year; and therefore the contradiction is self-evident.

But, however this may be, notwithstanding the publication of the celebrated Collection of Francanzano, in 1507, the *Cosmographiæ Introductio*, printed the same year in Lorraine, and other writings anterior to Vespucius's letters above cited, the authors to whom we are indebted for the beautiful edition of Ptolemy, published at Rome in the year following, 1508, (Marco Beneventano and Cotta,[2]) not only say nothing of Vespucius and his fictitious voyages, but, on the contrary, declare that the New Continent was discovered by Columbus and the Portuguese. All that is found in their production, particularly the dissertation of Beneventano, and also the chapters 3d and 14th, is in favor of the Portuguese navigators, as will be elsewhere explained. In the third chapter we read as follows; "*De Tellure quam tum Columbus, tum Lusitani, observaverunt, quam terram Sanctæ-Crucis appellant.* (Concerning the land which Columbus and the Portuguese discovered, to which they give the name of Santa Cruz.)" &c. &c. And we desire here pointedly to acknowledge the valu-

[1] Collection of Francanzano and others.

[2] We have examined this edition at the Royal Library.

able ideas we have met with in this work, which, having been published during the lifetime of Vespucius, and subsequently to the collections already quoted, adds to the proofs that can be adduced in opposition to the pretensions of this navigator, and the documents published in his interest. Hardly was our examination of it finished when the learned result of M. de Humboldt's [1] labors came under our notice; and we lose no time in here producing the observations of this illustrious *savant*, whose authority in the matter is, with so great reason, both powerful and decisive. He says, "I have found in the splendid edition of the Geography of Ptolemy, published at Rome in 1508, *proofs of the Portuguese navigation along the east coasts of South America, which was extended to the fiftieth degree of south latitude*, accompanied, however, at the same time, by the reflection that the extremity of the continent had not yet been attained. This edition, printed by Evangelista Tossinus, and composed by Marco Beneventano and John Cotta of Verona, contains a *mappemonde* (world-map) by Ruysch,[2] in which South America is represented as an island of immense extent, under the name of *Terra Sanctæ Crucis, sive Mun-*

1 Examen Critique de l' Histoire de la Geographie du Nouveau Continent. Paris. 1837. Vol. ii. pp. 5, 9.

2 Nova et Universalior Orbis cogniti Tabula, a Johanne Ruysch, Germano, elaborata.

*dus Novus.* (The Land of the Holy Cross,[1] or New World.) One sees there the Cape of the Holy Cross; it occupies the position of St. Augustine; and the coast is seen running to the South. A note is attached, which may be translated as follows: — *Portuguese mariners discovered this part of this territory, and proceeded as high as the fiftieth degree of south latitude, but without reaching its southern extremity.*

"The same edition presents a dissertation with this title: *Nova orbis descriptio, ac nova oceani navigatio, quâ Lisbonâ ad Indicum pervenitur pelagus; a Marco Beneventano, monacho Cœlestino, edita.* (A new description of the world and a new ocean navigation, by which the passage from Lisbon to the Indies is made known; published by Marco Beneventano, a Celestine Monk.)

"The 14th chapter reads; — *Terra Sanctœ Crucis decrescit usque ad latitudinem* 37° *aust.; quamque ad Archiploi usque ad* 50° *austr. navigarint, ut ferunt; quam reliquam portionem descriptam non reperi,* etc."

The learned author adds that the discovery of Brazil by Cabral, from the tenth to the sixteenth and a half degree of southern latitude, had made

[1] We beg the reader to pay particular attention to this denomination, employed after the famous Lorraine edition of the *Cosmographiœ Introductio.*

such an impression on the minds of men that the Court of Lisbon, subsequently to that event, even extended its views to the discovery of a western passage; and, to use his own words, "it consequently appears quite probable, that there took place, between 1500 and 1508, a succession of Portuguese attempts to the south of Porto Seguro, along the *Terra Sanctæ Crucis*, and that vague notions of these attempts have served as a foundation for a multitude of marine charts, which were fabricated in the most frequented seaports."

We will here give a chronology of the voyages made by the Portuguese to the *Terra Sanctæ Crucis*, (Brazil,) from the time of its discovery by Cabral to the year 1506, in order to show that the editors of the Ptolemy of 1508 were doubtless aware of the truth, and that, having a most accurate knowledge of the principal events, to wit, the results of these Portuguese expeditions, they preserved, designedly it is probable, *a profound silence respecting the pretended voyages and discoveries of Vespucius in* 1501 *and* 1503. These chronological notes will serve likewise to establish the reality of a series of attempts by the Portuguese, such as have been sagaciously supposed by M. de Humboldt to have taken place.

1501.—An expedition commanded by Gonçalo Coelho, left Lisbon to explore the coast of the *Terra de Santa Cruz*. Galvao, a contemporary author, says that this expedition, having recognized the Brazilian coast towards the fifth degree of latitude, sailed along the shore as far as the thirty-second degree south.[1]

1503. — After the return of the expedition just described, another was sent from Portugal, composed of six vessels, and commanded by Christovao Jaques, who reconnoitred and explored the coast as far as the *Cap das Virgens*, at the entrance of Magellan's Straits.[2] This Christovao Jaques is the same who discovered *Bahia de todos os Sanctos*. (San Salvador.)[3]

1503, June 10th. — The time of Gonçalo Coelho's second expedition. Goes says that the king, Emmanuel, sent this captain to reconnoitre the land of *Santa Cruz*, and that he sailed from Lisbon the 10th of June, with six vessels.[4] Osorio, too, also a contemporary, remarks, "*He (the king) committed the fleet to Gonçalo Coelho, for the purpose of making a survey of the country explored by Cabral, which they call Brazil.*"

1503. — In this same year the celebrated captain, Alfonso de Albuquerque, with a fleet bound from Lisbon to the Indies, reconnoitred the coast of Brazil, and cast anchor there.[5]

1 See the Portuguese writers, and especially Corografia Brazilica.
2 See Corografia Brazilica.
3 See Goes, Chron , and the last named authority.
4 Ibid.
5 See Ramusio, and Corografia Brazilica.

1505. — The fleet commanded by Don Francisco de Almeida, who sailed from Lisbon for the Indies, the 25th of March, with twenty vessels, ran along and surveyed the coast of Santa Cruz. (Brazil.)[1]

1506. — Tristam da Cunha, in command of a fleet of eleven vessels bound to the Indies, left Lisbon the sixth of March, went to examine Brazil, and sailed by a part of the coast of that country.[2]

The perfect accordance of the dates and objects of these expeditions with the very words of Beneventano's dissertation in the edition of Ptolemy, (1508,) and with the history of the time, shows, — 1st, that the editors of that work were intimately acquainted with this series of voyages, *which were conducted entirely by the Portuguese;* 2d, that the friendly terms which were sustained between Portugal and the Holy See, facilitated the immediate and regular communication of ideas the most precise upon discoveries in which the Court of Rome took a great interest; and 3d, that the succession of expeditions of which we have given a list, should suffice to demonstrate the falseness of the narrations of Vespucius. For it is evident, that if indeed he had discovered the Brazilian coast during his two pretended voyages of 1501 and 1503, it would have been useless to send at the same time, and at a later

[1] See Corografia Brazilica, vol. i. p. 44, and contemporary authors.

[2] Castanheda, Book ii. chap. 32, and Corografia Brazilica.

period, other expeditions exclusively Portuguese for the purpose of making the same exploration, to discover what had already been found out, and to verify that which was no longer doubtful.

The letter of Pedro Vaz Caminha, who sailed with Cabral, addressed from the New Continent, the first of May, 1500, to the king, Emmanuel, is of no little importance in the matter before us. The original of this valuable document, the details of which are very curious, is preserved in the royal archives at Lisbon, and it has been published by M. Ayres de Cazal, in his *Brazilian Chorography*.[1] A critical comparison of this letter and of Galvao's narrations, which we shall presently cite, with the letters attributed to Vespucius, will be sufficient, in our opinion, to determine the appellation that should be applied to the latter. By means of this letter we perceive how utterly void of foundation is the conjecture of the Chevalier Napione[2]; for in it are found the names of all those who accompanied Cabral in this expedition, *and that of Vespucius is not there.* This same letter, too, we have compared with an account of Cabral's voyage written by a Portuguese pilot, and inserted in the collection of Ramusio, which follows that of Madrignano.

In a relation of the voyages of Lodovico di Barthema of Bologna, we observe that this navigator

[1] Corografia Brazilica, vol. i. p. 12.

[2] Esame Critico del Primo Viaggio di Amerigo Vespucci.

went to sea in the service of King Emmanuel, that he returned from the Indies to Portugal on board the vessel of a Florentine, Bartholomew Marchioni, of whom Barros, Goes, and the Venetian Envoy speak, and that he reached Lisbon in 1507; but we nowhere find any allusion to either Vespucius or his discoveries.

We would also call attention to the silence of Castanheda,[1] a contemporary author, who while discoursing of the discoveries made by Cabral, and especially by the companions of that admiral, *never mentions Vespucius.*[2] The same silence is observed by Barreiros, likewise a contemporary, who speaks only of Columbus, in his treatise *De Ophira Regione*, which was printed at Coïmbra in 1560, and is found in the *Novus Orbis*, published at Rotterdam in 1616. The same is true, too, of Galvao, author of a work called *Descobrimentos Antigos e Modernos*, who lived at the time, and was a witness of the expeditions we are examining; likewise of *Pedro de Magalhaes de Gandavo*, the oldest historian of Brazil. The latter author in his *History of the Province of Santa Cruz*, first printed at Lisbon in 1576, *declares Cabral* to have been the discoverer of Brazil, without referring in the slightest manner either to Vespucius or to his imaginary voyages of 1501 and 1503. Yet Magalhaes merited and

1 Historia da Conquista da India pelos Portugueses.

2 See the curious reflections of Napione. Esame Critico, p. 84.

received the praises of the great poet, Camoëns; because he availed himself, in his work, of the most authentic sources of information. And could it, then, have been possible that he knew nothing of the books of voyages published in Lorraine, at Vienna, Venice, Paris, and elsewhere? We are not of that opinion.

The author of the *Corografia Brazilica*, while complaining of the falseness of Vespucius's narratives, cleverly remarks, that their very identity with those of Galvao stamps them as forgeries. And we will further point out the silence of Father Joseph Teixeira, who, although in his work entitled *De Portugalliæ Ortu, Regni Initiis*, etc., he gives a summary of the remarkable events in the reign of King Emmanuel, and at the epoch of Vespucius's would-be discoveries, says not a word of the Florentine navigator. And we would ask if this author, whose works are very numerous and nearly all printed at Paris towards the end of the sixteenth century, could have been ignorant of the pretensions of Vespucius, and even have known nothing of his letters, when the point in discussion was the Florentine's voyages, made by order of the king, Emmanuel?

Thus, it appears that in the Portuguese historians of the sixteenth century, the name of Vespucius is never found; and that no one at Rome should have been acquainted with his letters seems incredible, as is justly observed by Napione;[1] who owns, that if no mention is made of them in the *Itinerarium Portugallensium*, published in 1508,[2] nor by Albertino,[3] nor Giraldini,[4] and other contemporary authors,[5] this silence ought to convince us that these writers *did not regard them as genuine*. He admits, too, that Guicciardini, Segni, and others, who have spoken of the event, and many Italian authors besides, have never attributed the discoveries in question to Vespucius, and adds that he has not met with any Tuscan *savant* or old Florentine historian, who maintained that the American continent was discovered by their countryman in advance of Columbus.

The opinion of Guicciardini, it must be remembered, is of vast importance in this discussion; for he was a Florentine, and contemporary of Vespucius; he had been Spanish ambassador at the court of Ferdinand the Catholic, and was, moreover, bound by family ties to the Medici, one of whom, Leo the 10th, called him to Rome. He made himself useful to

1 Esame Critico, page 38.

2 This is an error of Napione, as we have ascertained by an examination of the compilation, which is not contained in the Royal Library, but a copy of which was obligingly loaned to us by M. Jomard. Another is to be found at the library of the Institute.

3 In 1510.

4 See his Itinerary of 1516, and Zeno, Diss. Vossiane.

5 See Napione, (Esame Critico,) upon the *Portulan*, (Description of Seaports, etc.) printed at Venice in 1528, which, though speaking of Columbus, says not a word of Vespucius.

Alessandro de' Medici, and, after the death of that prince, powerfully contributed to the election of Cosmo, of the same family. And amid a concurrence of circumstances like these, is it credible that a historian so celebrated as he was could have remained in ignorance of Vespucius's pretensions, and of the existence of his letters to Lorenzo Pier de' Medici, or that he would have proclaimed Columbus in the manner he did, if in his opinion the accounts of his own countryman had been worthy of belief? His manner of speaking of Columbus, and the Portuguese and Spanish discoveries, betrays, we think, his hesitation respecting the claims of the Florentine. For he asserts that Columbus first discovered the New Continent, and that Vespucius went to it also,[1] but, adds he (*dopo lui*) after Columbus. And he goes on immediately to say, that many others visited it likewise, and that they discovered *other islands, and most extensive countries on terra firma.* Now, if the navigators who, before 1504 and after Vespucius, accomplished great discoveries on the main land, took no part in the expeditions of that Florentine, it evidently follows that the historian meant it to be understood that *terra firma* was not discovered by him, — an opinion which seems to us yet more clearly expressed in the very next words of the text: "*Praise be to those Portuguese and Spaniards, and*

[1] It is probable that he here means the voyage with Hojeda.

*above all to Columbus, the discoverer of this most wonderful and dangerous navigation*, etc. etc.

Bernardo Segni, an Italian historian, born at Florence towards the end of the fifteenth century, was, like Guicciardini, a countryman and contemporary of Vespucius and his fabulous discoveries. He was at the head of a commercial house, and must necessarily have been well acquainted with the field of discovery which such vast regions as had lately been made known, laid open to adventurous expeditions. He made himself serviceable to the Medicean family, and the Duke, Cosmo de' Medici, confided to him a diplomatic mission to Ferdinand, king of the Romans, who was on intimate terms with the Court of Portugal.[1] Segni was afterwards appointed to be chief of the Academy, (*de la Crusca*,) and died at Florence in 1558. How then is it possible that this Florentine author, who lived and wrote in the time of Vespucius, who had the principal direction of a commercial establishment, who had visited Germany, where the letters of Vespucius were already known, — how is it possible that he could have been ignorant of this person's claims to priority in the discovery of the New Continent?

Ramusio himself, while inserting in his collection the so-called voyages of Vespucius, says, in his pre-

[1] See the *Corps Diplomatique*, section 24, by the author, M. de Santarem.

face to the expedition of the Portuguese, Francisco Alvares, in Ethiopia, that his narrative *should not be held in less esteem than those which we have already enjoyed by means of the discovery of Columbus.*

Hakluyt, in his dedicatory epistle to Sir Robert Cecil, calls Columbus the first navigator who, in 1492, discovered the New World; notwithstanding what he relates of Madoc, and notwithstanding Vespucius's pretensions.

Besides, there is an ancient monument, still to be seen at Saint Paul, in Brazil, which affords, respecting the subject now before us, an additional proof of high importance. At the entrance of the bar of *Cananea*, on the continental side, and upon a pile of stones, is found a pedestal of European marble, four hand-breadths in height, two in width, and one hand-breadth square. Cut upon it, are the arms of Portugal; but the towers are wanting; and, according to the author of the *Brazilian Chorography*,[1] there is yet visible the date, 1503, which proves to a certainty, in his opinion, that the fleet sent that year, for the purpose of examining and exploring *la Terra de Santa Cruz*, did not get as far as eighteen degrees of south latitude, as Vespucius alleges; because, if it had it must necessarily have left landmarks resembling the arms of Portugal, and of the

[1] Ayres de Cazal, Corografia Brazilica, published in 1817, vol. i. p. 2[illegible].

same date, in order to ratify the act of taking possession, according to the custom of the times.[1]

The same author,[2] analyzing with a judicious criticism the marine expeditions of Vespucius, observes that his first letter, as well as the summary attributed to him, upon the pretended voyage of 1501, present nothing but inconsistencies, contradictions, and errors beyond endurance, at the same time that they are perfectly mute on those essential points which are never forgotten by a navigator, *leading one to suppose that Vespucius never went to Brazil at all.* And, moreover, that the account contained in his second letter, upon the expedition of 1503, is diametrically opposed to contemporary history, and nothing better than a tissue of barefaced falsehoods; that it lacks accuracy in indicating the fleet's destination, disguises events, substitutes absurd fables for facts, and, in a word, designedly suppresses the truth. In the opinion, too, of the author we quote, it seems highly improbable that a foreigner would have been sent for by the king of Portugal to command his ships when already more than one expedition had been under the guidance of Portuguese pilots; that to the land of Labrador, for example, that of Vasco di Gama, of Cabral, of Gaspar de Lemos, and of others besides.

1 This custom is proved by a great number of writers of the fifteenth and sixteenth centuries.

2 See note No. 1. p. 90.

"The customs pertaining to pilotage," says M. de Humboldt,[1] "which prevailed in the grand expeditions of Columbus, Gama, and Magellan, and which appear to us of so uncertain a character, would have been the admiration, I will not say merely of the mariners of Phœnicia, Carthage, and Greece, but even of the able navigators of Catalonia, the Basque Provinces, of Dieppe, and Venice, in the thirteenth and fourteenth centuries."

Las Casas in 1502, (*and this date is very important*,) had in his possession letters written by Columbus, upon the marks or proofs of *western lands, collected together by Portuguese pilots*.[2]

These facts, and many others which we omit for lack of space, show in what estimation should be held the complaints of Vespucius against the ignorance of Portuguese pilots and mariners, when, in the relation of his fabulous voyage of 1501, by way of displaying his cosmographical acquirements, he speaks as follows: — "It must here be remarked that this place is still about seven hundred leagues from Cape Vert, and that I calculate on having sailed more than eight hundred, on account of what we suffered from the tempestuous and changeable state of the weather, which was invariably hostile to us, *as also from the ignorance of the pilot, — a sort*

[1] Examen Critique sur l'Histoire de la Geographie du Nouveau Continent, vol. i. page 9.

[2] Ibid. vol. i. page 21.

*of people who are always the cause of long voyages.* So that we arrived in such a place, that if I had not been acquainted with Cosmography there would have been an end of us, especially as we had not a pilot who could tell within fifty leagues where we were. There we were, wandering about, now on this side and now on that, without knowing our course, when I all at once provided for my own safety and that of my companions by means of my astrolabe, quadrant, and other astrological instruments; which caused me to be highly honored by all hands, to such a degree, indeed, that from that time I was held by them in that esteem with which *the learned* are always regarded by good men, because I taught them the way of really navigating well, and, in fact, did so much, that they all acknowledge that ordinary pilots, ignorant of cosmography in comparison with me, would never have known how to make this passage."

Is it not evident, if this description of events be true, that the fault lay with him who, in spite of his cosmographical science and his influence in the expedition, allowed the ignorance of a pilot to prolong the voyage, "running now in one direction and now in another"? And why did he make use of his astrolabe and his knowledge only when death stared them in the face? Can any one believe, after having read what has gone before, that the pilots "could not tell within fifty leagues, where they were," —

that those who had been brought up in the excellent school of Sagres, men who had traversed the ocean so often, could have been so profoundly ignorant?

The valuable collection of *Portulans*, written in Portuguese at the beginning of the sixteenth century, which is in the Royal Library at Paris, proves the injustice of the Florentine navigator towards the Portuguese pilots and mariners whose reputation he desired to sacrifice that he might pedantically magnify his own nautical wisdom. This beautiful manuscript, now for the first time, perhaps, made known to the world, contains a series of observations, some of which go back as far as the year 1500.[1] In it, among other documents, we find, 1st, Tables for astronomical observations; 2d, The division and explanation of the tables, with the manner of using them; 3d, The rule of calculation for reducing leagues to degrees; the manner of calculating the latitude and longitude, and of determining the variation of the compass; 4th, A treatise upon the magnetic needle; and 5th, the rule for finding the polar star by means of the needle, and also the Cross in the southern hemisphere, etc. etc.

The pilots, André Pires, Pero Martins, and Guanchimo, among others, were the authors of these *Portulans*, and they notice the acquaintance with the globe possessed by the ancient geometricians. It is

[1] See the notice given by the author in the Supplement, cod. 7, 168-33.

probable that they referred to Posidonius of Rhodes, followed by Ptolemy, and to Eratosthenes, followed by Strabo, &c.; at all events, they established the theory pursued by Bartholomew Dias, which they recommend as the most accurate.[1]

These details are sufficient to show how unjustly was the reproach of ignorance cast at the Portuguese pilots by Vespucius; for it is most obvious, 1st, that the pilots who were the contemporaries of that Florentine had attained the most extensive cosmograhpical instruction peculiar to their epoch, and that they made use of the astronomical ephemeris of Regiomontanus; as any one can ascertain by inspecting carefully what is said by Barros and Amoretti in the introduction to the treatise on navigation by Pigafetta; and 2d, it is equally obvious that their observations were based upon the most ancient authorities, not excepting the Portuguese, as, for example, upon those of Bartholomew Dias, in 1486, when he discovered the *Cabo Tormentoso*, since called the Cape of Good Hope.[2]

[1] In the Cosmographical works of the Portuguese pilots, there is no respect for judicial astrology. It will be seen that the *Tractatus Spheræ*, by Andalo Nigro, had not the slightest influence on these authors, any more than the writings of the celebrated Thomas of Pisa. Nor do we find in these productions the vagaries of the astronomers of the middle age, in their astrological dreams. It rather seems that the works of the famous Picus of Mirandola, against judicial astrology, had already exerted a great influence upon the Portuguese cosmographers.

[2] The manuscripts could furnish us with more ample details, but they would divert us from our subject.

Neither in this collection of *Portulans*, nor in the remarks of two other Portuguese pilots,[1] Emmanuel Alvares and Ayres Fernandez, (who were also of the sixteenth century, between 1525 and 1550,) is to be found the slightest notice of the observations of Vespucius. Now, if Vespucius, by means of his cosmographical knowledge had been able, as he says, to save the expedition of 1501, and on that account was regarded by Portuguese mariners as a *savant* of the first order, is it to be presumed that the authors of the *Portulans*, by whom the greater part of this work was digested in the very lifetime of Vespucius, would have forgotten the observations made by so great a cosmographer? — observations the more important since, according to him, they were the salvation of a fleet! The study of geographers and historians, both Greek and Roman, was then, (in the fifteenth and sixteenth centuries,) cultivated with an extraordinary enthusiasm by the Portuguese, on account of the continual progress made in discovery and geographical knowledge among them, consequent upon the Arabian rule, which had widely spread the literary productions of the ancients and a taste for geography. M. Dacier, in a report made in the name of the Institute, has vividly set forth the immense utility there would be, in causing the

[1] Manuscripts in the Royal Library, No. 8, 172 – 3, Colbert Collection.

earliest Portuguese and Italian maps of the thirteenth and fourteenth centuries[1] to be engraved, so as to show what influence upon European discoveries in Africa the geographical knowledge of the Arabs had had. As to ourselves, the comparative study of Portuguese maps and narratives, and of works anterior to the fifteenth century, has furnished us with the most positive proof of the influence which the perusal of ancient geographers, and of navigators of the thirteenth and fourteenth centuries, had on the marine expeditions of the Portuguese and upon their distant discoveries.

The celebrated prince Don Pedro, duke of Coïmbra, son of king John I., who had visited the East, and received from the sultan of Babylon and from Amurat II. marks of their esteem, who had profoundly studied the Greek and Latin classics, and who maintained with Angelo Poliziano (Politian) and other learned men, relations of an intimate nature, brought to Lisbon a copy of the voyages of Marco Polo, which had been presented to him at Venice. And, on the other hand, his illustrious brother, the infant Don Henry, gave to voyages and cosmographical studies the most astonishing impulse, and that, too, long before the time of Vespucius. The pilots, who doubtless studied at the school of navigation at Sagres, attained a degree of knowledge

[1] Rapport au Nom d' l' Institut, p. 190.

which even now surprises us. And these facts authorize us to allege that the recriminations of Vespucius are void of justice, and the facts he cites equally wanting in accuracy.

We will continue to fortify our own conclusions by the opinions of a number of other writers whom we have not yet quoted. The author of a work called, *Novus Orbis, seu India Occidentalis,* (The New World, or the Western India,) etc., which was published in 1621, declares Columbus to have been the discoverer of the New Continent, without so much as once alluding to Vespucius. He complains of the wrong already committed against the former, and, speaking of the newly-found land, says: "It was first discovered by Christopher Columbus, a Genoese, in the year, &c. &c. . . . . . as well as other islands and countries of this New World, although some persons most unjustly and invidiously, but at the same time vainly, deny Columbus this honor," &c. &c.

Father Seraphino de Freitas, a Portuguese writer of the century just mentioned, in his book, *De justo Imperio Lusitanorum Asiatico* (concerning the legitimate Asiatic Empire of the Portuguese,) printed at Valladolid in 1625, without mentioning Vespucius, says of Columbus: *Christopher Columbus discovered the Indies.* And, moreover, if we examine the opinions of many authors of the eighteenth century, as yet unnoticed by us, we shall find them in like manner hostile to the Florentine navigator. Stuvenio, for example, in his *De vero Novi Orbis Inventore Dissertatio Historico-critica*, published at Frankfort in 1714, is in no way favorable to the pretensions of Vespucius.

Prévost did not insert in his collection the narratives of Vespucius, *because he did not consider them as sufficiently worthy of confidence.* And in the *Histoire Générale des Voyages*,[1] we read as follows: "The narrations given by Americus Vespucius contain an account of two voyages which he made on the same coast (Brazil) in the name of Emmanuel, King of Portugal; *but the dates of them are false, and therein consists the fraud.* For it is proved by all contemporary testimony that, at the time referred to, he was employed in other expeditions."

The learned journalists of Trévoux vigorously refuted, from the moment of its appearance, Bandini's book, in which he attempts the defence of Vespucius.[2] In our quotations from them we shall show in what light this apology was regarded by the critics, who thus express themselves: "Hojeda sailed with Americus Vespucius in 1499, as was juridically proved on oath by Hojeda himself and Andres de Morales, one of his pilots, when Don Diego Columbus, son and successor of Christopher, commenced a prosecution against Vespucius,[3] who, for the sake of

[1] Vol. xiv. book 6, chap. 9.

[2] Mémoires de Trévoux, Septembre 1746, article 93.

[3] The editors did not well understand this affair about the suit insti-

fixing his name on the New World, saw fit to proclaim that he had discovered the Continent in 1497, antedating his first voyage by two years, or rather, making two out of one, with attendant circumstances, which Hojeda and Morales declared to be false. A final decree of the royal Council of the Indies followed, establishing the fraud of Vespucius, which being the case, and the legitimate proofs of it being yet preserved in the archives of the said Council, what reliance can be placed on the accounts we have received of the two first voyages of this navigator, and how great suspicion should attach itself to his other writings, according to the maxim of Phædrus:

"Who by base fraud has once acquired a fame,
Not truth itself for him can credit gain."

"Antonio de Herrera, the great historian of the Indies, who studiously analyzed the documents in the Archives of the Council, informs us that Hojeda in 1502 made a second voyage to America, accompanied by Vespucius. Here, then, is an *alibi* distinctly pronounced against what is found in the last portion of the Abbé Bandini's collection, where the

tuted by the Council against the heirs of Christopher Columbus. See Navarrete, Coleccion de los Viages, vol. iii. pp. 5, 539. This suit was begun by the king's treasury against Don Diego Columbus, son of the admiral. We have been acquainted with these documents only a little while, and that through extracts of Muñoz and Navarrete. Vol. iii. pp. 559, 560, 595. So that there must have bee n an error on the part of the compilers of the Mémoires de Trévoux. Nevertheless, we have thought it advisable to transcribe this part of the article, as an additional proof of what we have before said.

author pretends that Vespucius left Lisbon [1] for Brazil in 1501, whence he did not return till the month of September, 1504. Bandini says that the King of Spain, delighted with the success of Vespucius, caused him to equip three vessels for the purpose of discovering the Trapobane in the Indian sea, but that, the king of Portugal having induced him to enter his service, he secretly betook himself to Lisbon,[2] where the King Emmanuel provided him with three vessels, and whence he sailed the 10th of May, 1501, steering for Africa, and that he made a second voyage to the same course in 1503. But how does this agree with the voyage to Brazil in 1501, which lasted three years, and with the second voyage of Hojeda's to the West Indies in 1501 and 1502? Bandini himself seems not a little embarrassed in arranging all these accounts, for, in his fourth chapter is found a digression, the object of which is to ascertain to what personage were addressed the letters of Vespucius. *But something surer than even the thread of Ariadne was necessary to save him from this labyrinth.*" [3]

The same critics remark in another place that,

[1] The "Art de vérifier les Dates," vol. xii. p. 115, fixes the departure of Vespucius and Hojeda the same year, 1501.

[2] In this Bandini contradicts Vespucius's letters. See the affair of the letters patent which he pretended he received from the king of Portugal, etc. etc.

[3] We have elsewhere examined this point. See the *Bulletin de la Société Géographique*, Septembre, 1836, pp. 138, 159, 160, 161.

"the list of writers, almost all Italians, and for the most part Florentines, from whom proceed these pompous eulogies of Vespucius, fills up the seventh and last chapter of his life; but in it not a single authority upon the historical point before us is to be discovered, which can affect, however slightly, the proofs that array themselves against the Florentine navigator."[1]

If the critique of the *Journal de Trévoux* is severe, the expressions of Claret de Fleurieu, in his *Observations sur la Division Hydrographique du Globe*,[2] are not less remarkable in our present discussion.

"No part of the east coast of America," says he, "bears the name of Columbus, who discovered it. When one surveys the eastern shore of the New World, bordered by the Atlantic and approaching the equator, it is with a sort of indignation that he can discover neither island, nor cape, nor a single point of this immense territory which is called after the hero navigator who discovered the continent, as he had previously the islands. Columbus is unheard

[1] This article of the *Mémoires de Trévoux*, although hardly cited by Napione, has nevertheless received the praises of this distinguished writer, who says, *Esame Critico del primo Viaggio del Vespucci*, p. 18:—"Very differently from Father Richa judged his learned brothers, the authors of the *Journal de Trévoux*, who, as soon as the life and letters of Vespucius appeared in print, strenuously opposed the opinions of Bandini, and sustained the cause and incontestable rights of Columbus."

[2] In the fourth volume of the *Voyages d' Etienne Marchand*, Paris, 1799, p. 25.

of and unseen, while an adventurer, *Americus Vespucius, embarked in what capacity nobody can tell, under the orders of Alonzo de Hojeda*, and visiting a part of the Continent subsequently to its discovery, succeeded in attaching to it forever his own name! He audaciously announced himself to all Europe as the first discoverer of the Continent of the New World, and deluded Europe, without examining, gave credit to his assertion! Men soon accustomed themselves to call the fourth part of the earth — a part far surpassing every other in extent — by the name of an impostor, who said he had discovered it and was believed; and this name usurped the place which the genius, courage, and perseverance of Columbus had legitimately acquired for his own! But unhappily time has sanctioned this usurpation, and the injustice done can no longer be remedied. *Yet the revival of its memory is to render to the immortal hero who suffered the wrong a reparation, which springs from posterity in revenge of the ingratitude he endured from his contemporaries.*" [1]

We will now turn to the opinion of a very learned man, who, by order of the Spanish government, devoted a portion of his life to the study of documents which related to the history of the discovery of the New Continent; we mean the historian Muñoz.[2]

[1] The author of this angry passage was not ignorant of the publication of the Abbé Bandini in favor of Vespucius, for he cites it in a note.

[2] Historia del Nuevo Mundo, by J. Bant. Muñoz, Madrid.

He says, "that there are no other published accounts of those navigators who continued the discoveries of Columbus up to 1500, except the narratives of the *famous Vespucius*, from whom the New Continent took its name ; and that these narratives, often printed, and finally brought together into one collection by Bandini in 1745, *have only served to complete the proofs of the impostures of their author*, as in another place I will show." [1]

"Nevertheless," the same author remarks, "I ought not to *pass by in silence this instance of successful cheating. Vespucius, regarded as a mariner, was vastly inferior to almost all the navigators of his time;* and yet he was better rewarded than any of them ; his memory, even to our day, having been cherished with all but the same homage as that which Columbus's has received. Even after a thousand learned writers have stripped this Florentine impostor of his mask, he still finds apologists ; and who can tell if human frailty may not yet bring forth imitators of Bandini and Felicé, who in their desire to sustain the mendacious glory of their hero by the aid of fiction, promising all the while authentic documents, have come to us citing the authority of *Moreri?*"

Camus, whose peculiar study was collections of voyages, although he had it not in his power to ex-

[1] Muñoz having published only his first volume, was unable to fulfil his promise.

amine that of Vicenza, thus expresses himself when speaking of the relations of Vespucius: "*I declare that there is here a great deal of uncertainty, and but a slight stamp of authenticity;*" and further on,[1] he adds, "*Americus Vespucius has in this respect usurped a glory which did not belong to him.*"

Peuchet, in the introduction to his *Dictionnaire de la Géographie Commerçante*, observes that in forming an estimate of Vespucius's pretensions, he will say, with Voltaire, that the glory of having discovered the New World incontestably belongs to him who had the genius and courage to undertake the first voyage. The honor, as Newton in his dispute with Leibnitz remarks, is due to the discoverer alone. Those who follow are only disciples. Columbus had already made three voyages with the rank of admiral, five years before Americus Vespucius, under the command of Hojeda, made a single one in the capacity of geographer.[2]

*Formaleone*, in his *Saggio sulla Nautica antica de' Veneziani*, exclaims, "This insolent Florentine, Americus Vespucius, robbed Columbus of the glory of giving his name to the New World."

Cladera, in his *Investigaciones Historicas sobre*

[1] Mémoires sur la Collection des grands and petits Voyages, etc. p. 164.

[2] Contemporary documents do not show in what capacity he accompanied Hojeda.

*los Principales Descobrimientos*, is of the same opinion with the historian Herrera, and in direct opposition to the pretensions of the panegyrists of Vespucius.

And, finally, M. de Humboldt, in his *Examen de l'Histoire de la Géographie du Nouveau Continent*, whenever he alludes to the expeditions attributed to Vespucius, declares again and again how problematical he considers them. "If it be true," are the words of this illustrious *savant*,[1] "that Vespucius saw, *in that which he calls his third voyage*, (between May, 1501, and September, 1502,) what he says he did, the constellation of the Great Bear at the horizon, he must have got to about the twenty-sixth degree of south latitude upon the eastern coast of America, *and not to the thirty-second as he himself affirms.*"

This being the manner in which the learned author treats of the fabulous third voyage of Vespucius, respecting the second we find what follows:[2] "Vespucius, *in his pretended* second expedition of 1499, calls by the name of Antillia the island which Columbus had discovered a few years before, that is, Hayti." Somewhat further, he continues,[3] "I have not found in the letters of Vespucius the conjunction of the moon and Mars, which ought to have been observed by that navigator in 1499." And

1 Vol. i. p. 57. 2 Vol. i. p. 251.
3 Ibid. p. 275.

again,[1] speaking of clandestine voyages,[2] he says, "It is to this sort of expeditions, *perhaps*, that those also belong which Vespucius must have made for the king, between 1501 and 1504, upon the coast of Brazil, although the pilot Vasco Garcia,[3] who designed the maps of western America, having received from Vespucius the true latitude of Cape Saint Augustine, remarks, that if the Florentine voyager went there clandestinely and maliciously in the service of the Portuguese, he never would have ventured to boast of it in Spain."[4]

What the pilot Garcia suggests is truly sagacious; for, in fact, Vespucius would not have dared to make such a boast in Spain, where the laws of July 28th, 1500, and of June 8th, 1501, inflicted very serious penalties on those who undertook similar enterprises. If, then, his voyages, undertaken for a foreign sovereign, ever really took place, how did it happen that he returned to Spain subsequently to the ordinances of which we just spoke? And how could he have received the royal instructions of the 15th of September, 1506, which are copied by Muñoz? This is a still stronger proof of the falseness of the relations relative to the fictitious voyages of 1501 and 1503.

Expressions like the following are found in M. de Humboldt's work: — "Whatever doubts may be

[1] Ibid, pp. 355, 356. [2] See Navarrete, vol. iii.

[3] It must be remembered that this pilot was a Spaniard.

[4] See Navarrete, vol. iii. pp. 24, 32.

entertained *respecting Vespucius and his very problematical series of expeditions,*" &c. &c. . . . "*The contestable dates of Americus Vespucius's first letters*" &c. &c.[1] And in another place[2] he observes, "The only occasion on which the name of Columbus is found in the letters of Vespucius, is when it is mentioned in connection with Antillia." The author then, after citing the Latin text of the *Cosmografiæ Introductio*, adds, "These words are taken from the narrative of Vespucius's *pretended* second voyage, which he says he finished on the eighth of September, 1500. The connection of events proves that the name of Antillia was given by Vespucius to the island of Hispaniola, and that the account written *is that of the voyage he made with Hojeda;* for in the first feigned voyage, the commencement of which Vespucius says was the twentieth of May, 1497, Hispaniola is simply called Ity, a corruption without doubt of Aïti."

"Bartholomew di Las Casas," it is subsequently remarked by M. de Humboldt, "informs us that it was the Portuguese who applied by preference the name of Antillia to Hispaniola; and then, if Vespucius did not, as he himself asserts, embark in company with any Portuguese till 1501 and 1503, how came he to designate as Portuguese the pilots and mariners of his expedition in the narrative of

[1] Vol. ii. p. 3. [2] Ibid. p. 176.

his pretended voyage in 1497, that is, four years before his arrival in Portugal ? "

From all that we have brought to light and exposed, it appears to us the following facts may be deduced, supported, as they are, by a vast number of contemporary and other authorities, which have been examined and discussed according to the rules of true criticism : —

1. The discovery of the New Continent is due, without a doubt, to Columbus ; or, if he was not the first to discover this part of the world, he was, at least, the man who *re*-discovered it, and in a positive and definite shape communicated the knowledge of it. For, if he verified what the Egyptian priest indicated to Solon the Athenian, as is related by Plato in the Timæus, respecting the island of Atlantis ; if he realized the hypothesis of Ætian ; if he accomplished the prophecy of Seneca in the Medea ; if he demonstrated that the story of the mysterious Carthagenian vessel, related by Aristotle and Theophrastus, was not a dream ; if he established by deeds, that there was nothing visionary in what St. Gregory pointed at in one of his letters to St. Clement ; if, in a word, Columbus proved by his discovery, the existence of the land which Madoc had visited before him, as Hakluyt and Powell pretended, and ascertained to a certainty that which for the ancients had always been so uncertain, problematical, and mysterious, — his glory becomes only

the more splendid, and more an object to command admiration.

2. Priority in discovery of the eastern part of the New Southern Continent belongs to those Portuguese navigators who, by a series of expeditions, were the first to explore those immense regions.[1]

3. Americus Vespucius never commanded a single expedition; for, even in the second voyage of Hojeda, that of 1499 and 1500, he was only a subaltern. And that expedition, the only one which he seems to have had any share in, *confined itself to an examination of the coast of Venezuela*, and was

[1] The author of the *Corografia Brazilica*, (vol. i. p. 34,) says, *that the Spanish writers* pretend that their countryman, Vicente Yañez Pinzon, had recognized Cape St. Augustine, and given the name of Cape Consolation to it, three months before Cabral discovered Porto Seguro. And to prove that Cape St. Augustine and Cape Consolation are the same, they assert that Pinzon had viewed the land at a great distance, that the water of the sea was very muddy, whitish, and as sweet as river water, and that soundings were found at sixteen fathoms. But all these signs and all these particulars prove quite the contrary, and go to show that *Cape Consolation* was the *North Cape*, which is in the second degree of south latitude. The land of Cape St. Augustine, and the neighborhood of it, are flat, and can be seen only a short distance at sea; the waters in that locality are remarkably clear and transparent; and the lead marks sixteen fathoms only near shore. Nor can sweet water be found on this coast except in those rivers where the sea does not ascend. The same author acknowledges that Pinzon, having run forty leagues along this coast, ascertained that the sweet water issued from the river Maranpas, that is, the Amazon, whose mouth is more than four hundred leagues from St. Augustine. See also the remarks of Robertson, book ii., and better still, the deposition of Cabot, in 1518, before the council of pilots. See likewise the observations by the author, M. de Santarem, upon the celebrated map of Juan de la Cosa, drawn in 1500.

under the direction of the celebrated Biscayan pilot, Juan de la Cosa.

4. The voyages attributed to Vespucius being problematical, and destitute of those proofs which insure authenticity,[1] he has no claim to be classed among the first discoverers of the New Continent; for if among these are to take their places those who visited that region subsequently to Columbus and Cabral, then even Pinzon, (in 1499 and 1500,) Lope, (in 1500,) and De las Bastidas, (in 1501,) might dispute this honor with the Florentine, and with so much the more reason as they themselves were in chief command of the expeditions to which their names are attached.

A series of contemporary documents, taken from the royal archives of Simancas and Seville, and only very lately published, (1829,) establishes in the clearest possible manner, that Vespucius had been employed in catering for vessels, as had also Berardi; that, on the death of Berardi, in 1495, he succeeded him as purveyor; and that in this way he was occupied, without interruption, till 1499, when he embarked with Hojeda.[2] It further shows that he caused himself to be *naturalized in Spain*, in 1505;[3] and that he still continued commissioned to purchase the necessaries for vessels leaving Seville for the

[1] See the notes inserted by the author in the Bulletin of September, 1841.

[2] See the documents collected by Muñoz and Navarrete, vol. iii. Col. Diplom.

[3] Letters patent of April 24th. (Archives of Simancas.)

New World and the East Indies, in 1506 and 1507, which was the very moment when the famous *Cosmographiæ Introductio* and the pretended discoveries of the Florentine geographer were published in Lorraine under the pseudonym, Ilacomilus. The same series of documents informs us that Vespucius had been appointed boatswain's mate to a vessel called the *Medina*, for a voyage which never took place, and that too, several years after the discovery of the New World by Columbus, and a long while subsequently to this great man's receiving the rank of Admiral. Now, these documents, entirely unknown to Bandini and Father Canovai, the two apologists of the Florentine, confirm in the most positive manner the results which we have laid before our readers; and in them is not found the slightest mention of any discoveries whatever made by that navigator; and surely in his letters of naturalization, and in his patent of pilot-major, dated March 22d, 1508, if any discoveries had really been made by him, some allusion must have necessarily been made to them; but, on the contrary, in these papers nothing is met with except the formal terms peculiar to the chancellery. The conclusion from all which is, that previously to 1499 Vespucius had made not a single voyage of discovery, and that subsequently to that period his services were held in so slight consideration as to entitle him only to the simple rank of *pilot-major*, sixteen years after the discovery of the New Continent by Admiral Columbus.

We learn further from these documents, that in 1515 the observations of Vespucius were regarded as so little worthy of credit in Spain that, in a council of pilots which took place in that year for the purpose of determining the latitude of St. Augustine, Sebastian Cabot employed these words: — "*If any faith can be placed in the voyage which Americus says he made, &c. &c.*" And John Vespucius himself, nephew of Americus, and member of the council, while doing his utmost to give effect to the authority of his uncle upon the true latitude of the Cape, evidently indicates by his expressions, that he had not too much confidence in his relative's stories; for the termination of what he had to say was as follows: — "*If His Highness was desirous of verifying what Americus had said respecting the latitude of the Cape, he could determine its accuracy by sending a caravel there.*" The other pilots were ignorant of the subject: and Vasco Garcia, who was best disposed to Americus on this point, proved, by what he said, still more strongly, in our opinion, what faint confidence the narratives of Vespucius, relative to these voyages, merited.

We will finish this chapter by declaring, in the most positive manner and with the greatest sincerity, that in the present discussion it has not been our object to obscure or diminish in the least degree the immense renown which belongs to the country of Vespucius; but that, on the contrary, being en-

8

thusiastic in our admiration of that cradle of the arts and sciences, and birthplace of so many celebrated men, we should have easily hastened to proclaim Vespucius as one of that number, if such an honor had been legitimately due to his deserts. But the land of Dante and of the Medici stands in no need of a fame that has been usurped, nor of a grandeur which three centuries have disputed. We are certain, then, that no imputation will be cast upon us; for, if with a thousand other writers, some of them Italians, we have set ourselves in opposition to one native of Italy, we have at the same time defended the cause of another individual born in that country.

If there be any of our readers who yet entertain doubts on a point in the history of discovery so full of confusion and difficulty as that under consideration, we beg them to accompany us, while we demonstrate more fully than we have yet done, the errors and contradictions of Father Canovai, author of the eulogy on Vespucius; as we have already exposed those of Bandini, his other eulogist, therein being supported by the learned authors of the *Mémoires de Trévoux*, by the historian Robertson, the Chevalier Napione, and others.

No one, let it be remarked, in conclusion, has a right to alter and amend, as has been attempted, a certain portion of Vespucius's letters, wherein facts and dates are erroneously stated, for the sake of making them coincide with the existence of individuals to whom they were addressed; nor can there be, consistently with justice, a substitution of other facts, dates, and names, in the extraordinary expectation of procuring for these documents an authenticity and a stamp of veracity, which originally they never had. Such is the theme which we propose more fully to develop, as we proceed in this examination.

## CHAPTER V.

We have demonstrated, in the preceding chapters, 1. That not the slightest trace of Vespucius, nor a single document concerning him, or his problematical voyages of 1501 and 1503, is to be found in the royal archives of Portugal, notwithstanding all he says of himself, and of the invitation which the king Emmanuel gave him, on sending his letters patent; and, moreover, if he had spoken the truth, that such traces and documents should have existed in that national depository, at least while the historian Goes was living, in like manner as several documents concerning him are still extant in the archives of Timancas and Seville. 2. That all the Portuguese historians and geographers of the sixteenth century have preserved a profound silence respecting Vespucius, and his fabulous voyages of 1501 and 1503. 3. That Italian, and even Tuscan writers, scrupulously honest, and contemporaries, too, of the event, have universally declared that Columbus was the first who discovered the New Continent. And 4. We have shown by a great many documents and by critical analyses, the inconsistencies of Vespucius's narratives, and of the letters attributed to him. We have cited more than one hundred and fifty authorities, authors who wrote on voyages and discoveries; some of whom were contemporaries, and others adepts in the science of geographical history. With Navarrete we have exposed the absurdity of Vespucius's observations, the result of which would have been to put his vessels one hundred and sixty-five leagues in the interior of the Continent! and have exhibited the inconsistency of his taking possession of newly-found lands in the name of the king of Spain, when, according to his own account, the expedition was ordered by the king of Portugal. We have made manifest the incoherence of his story, by which it would appear that the number of his vessels dwindled down to a solitary bark, with a crew of only four or five sailors; and that, after having accomplished in it a voyage of three hundred leagues to Bahia, and a subsequent one of two hundred and sixty, he finished by leaving his vessel in port and returning to Lisbon! We have made evident the impossibility of his having written and addressed letters to a king who had been dead twenty-four years; and of his having been educated, as he pretends in his dedication to René of Lorraine, with a prince who was forty-two years old at the time of his birth! We have proved that his letters could not have been addressed to René II.; and have stated how difficult it is to believe that they were written either to Lorenzo Piero de' Medici, called the Magnificent, who was no longer alive at the time of Vespucius's voyages, or to Lorenzo II., who had not, when the first of these took place, yet attained his eighth year! We have established, by the rules of true criticism, that a single essential defect, which, morally speaking, could not have slipped into an authentic document, evinces the falseness of the writing where it is found; and that, consequently, the important errors both in history and chronology, which we have pointed out in the present case, conduce to a like conclusion. Equally true, too, is it, as we have shown, that an individual fact, which cannot be made to correspond with such and such personages and circumstances to which a document relates, is sufficient to condemn the said document as a forgery. We have explained, by an examination of the oldest and most rare collections of voyages, what weight was given to the report of Vespucius's pretended discoveries, by means of fraudulent title-pages; and, with contemporary works in hand, unedited manuscripts and documents very lately drawn from public archives, we have made known how many false judgments have been pronounced on Vespucius and his fabulous voyages. And now, after having done thus much, we will confine ourselves to certain observations, whose end will be to dissipate, if possible, the doubts of those who still permit themselves to be deluded by the mendacious pretensions of Vespucius's friends, by the panegyrists of his discoveries, and by the perusal of works which are the fruit of error and adulation.

Among more than two hundred productions which have passed under our examination, there are but two, — the two eulogies published by Bandini, and especially by Father Canovai, — that are wholly favorable to the pretensions of Vespucius. Bandini's work, as we have already said, so far from satisfying those who doubted the truth of Vespucius's narratives, or rather the narratives attributed to him, was, at the instant of its publication, refuted by the erudite compilers of the *Mémoires de Trévoux*, by Robertson and Napione, and has been constantly rejected by sound criticism. As to that of Canovai, although less violently attacked than Bandini's, it has never been regarded as an authority by conscientious geographers and writers who have consulted it, and its only merit consists in the greater quantity of materials it furnishes for refutation. Indeed, we cannot comprehend how any reliance can be placed on either of these works, after so many men, eminent for their historical investigations of voyages and discoveries, have exposed the errors and absurdities they contain, and after the exposure of these errors and absurdities (comprising points of fundamental importance) has been fully confirmed by documents recently brought to light.

It has been objected, in favor of Americus Vespucius, that Columbus kept silence respecting his own discoveries, and that even some mystery was made of them in Spain; while Vespucius, by publishing an account of his expeditions and discoveries, acquired at once a great celebrity. But, in answer to this, besides what has already been said, we will remark, that the voyages and discoveries of Columbus never bore a clandestine character, and that they were, immediately on their completion, known to all Europe, and, above all, to the Romans and Venetians. His letters, too, were published, previously to those imputed to Vespucius; for, in 1493, Leandro Cosco translated and published in Spanish one of them, which passed through three editions in the same year, — an unexampled instance, perhaps, at that epoch, as M. Ternaux well observes,[1] and one which testifies the general interest excited from the commencement of discovery by Columbus.

In the following year, Carlo Verardo, in a work entitled the *Conquest of Grenada*, (De Expugnatione Granatæ,) treated of the islands lately discovered in the Indian Ocean by Columbus. And in 1501, Angelo Trivigiaro, secretary to Domenico Pizani, the ambassador of the Venetian Republic in Spain, wrote to Domenico Malapiero, another nobleman of Venice, relative to Columbus's discoveries. It was also in 1504 that Alberto Vercellese, of Lisona, at the dictation of Trivigiaro, printed a small

[1] Bibliothèque Américaine.

work, now become very rare, having for its title: *Libretto di tutte le Navigatione dei Re' de Spagna, colle Isole e Terre nuovamente trovati.*[1]

If these facts are not sufficient to prove, beyond dispute, how universally published were the discoveries of Columbus, the moment he returned to Europe; and that no mystery whatever, either on his part or on that of the Spanish court, attached itself to the voyages made by him, from the time that the New Continent was discovered, the bull of Alexander VI. [addressed to Ferdinand and Isabella,] ought certainly to suffice, for in it are found the following expressions: — "Dilectum filium Christophorum Columbum, virum utique dignum et plurimum commendandum, ac tanto negotio aptum, cum navigiis et hominibus ad similia instructis, non sine maximis laboribus et periculis ac expensis destinastis, ut terras firmas et insulas remotas, et incognitas, hujusmodi, per mare ubi hactenus navigatum non fuerat, diligenter inquireret.[2] Qui tandem, divino auxilio, facta extrema diligentia, in mari Oceano navigantes, *certas insulas remotissimas et etiam terras firmas, quæ per alios hactenus repertæ non fuerant invenerunt*," etc.[3]

[1] See Bossy.

[2] Cladera, Investigaciones Históricas, p. 7.

[3] Cladera has cited only the first part of this important passage, and has not quoted correctly. We have copied from the document as given, entire, by Cancellieri, *Dissertazioni sopra Cristoforo Colombo*, p. 184. [It is proper to observe, that the text given above is that

Again, it was the custom of Columbus to address to different personages among his protectors letters whose contents were the same, almost to the very forms of expression,[1] — a peculiarity which ought to exclude all idea of any mysteriousness on his part as to the subject of discoveries. There can be no doubt, then, that the discoveries made by him were, from the moment of their completion, known to the European world, and that, consequently, he was the first to present himself in the character of discoverer of the New Continent. His silence, therefore, cannot be pleaded in justification of Vespucius, under the pretext that the latter presented his claims first, and that his letters were in universal circulation, while the discoveries of Columbus were wrapped up in a veil of mystery.

During the life of the great Genoese no one dared to impose upon the New Continent the name of America, notwithstanding the letters of Vespucius, written before the death of Columbus (1506); and, according to the supposition of M. de Humboldt, it was not till the following year that the thing was attempted, by the pseudonymous Ilacomilus. This particular claims the serious attention of

which appears in the *Magnum Bullarium Romanum*, (Lugduni, 1655,) tom. i. p. 466. Compare Navarrete, Coleccion de los Viages, tom. ii. p. 30, and Cancellieri, as already cited. M. de Santarem has copied Cancellieri very inaccurately.]

[1] Humboldt, Examen Critique, p. 338, note 2, large edition.

critics, because it is impossible to believe that such an injustice, as confounding the two navigators together, was committed by Ilacomilus through ignorance. That this anonymous writer, who was a *savant* of Friburg, in correspondence with Ringmann of Basle, and whom M. de Humboldt believes to have been the geographer Waldseemuller, (author of a German marine chart,) that one who travelled in Lorraine, occupying himself with geographical studies, and was in the neighborhood of Genoa, where the voyages and discoveries of Columbus had been for a long time known, as they were also in Italy and elsewhere, that such a one could have been ignorant of the reality of the discovery of the New Continent by Columbus, seems to us an absurdity to suppose, especially when we consider that the event had happened fourteen years before. Equally absurd is it to imagine that Ilacomilus knew nothing of Columbus's letters, of which there had been already three editions published, or that he had never heard of the work of Verardi, printed at Basle in 1494 by Bergmann de Olpe, particularly as he was in correspondence with the learned men of that place, and busied himself about geography and recent discoveries, as is shown by the influential part he took in the publication of the *Cosmographiæ Introductio*. And if we must admit that he had any connections with Vespucius, who was in Spain, for a still stronger reason we must affirm that he could not but have been acquainted with the discoveries of Columbus, and many others that were made in 1507, the year in which the *Introductio* was published. And as to Vespucius himself, if he had been as sincerely honest as it is pretended he was, why, when he was in relation with Ilacomilus by way of Lorraine, did he not object to the geographer's calling the New Continent by his name, to the prejudice of the fame of Columbus, his benefactor?

It cannot be alleged that Vespucius was ignorant of what was passing in Lorraine in respect to himself and his arrogation of another's glory, or that he was unaware of what his friend was doing for him; for this would be not only illogical, but the denial of the existence of the *Cosmographiæ Introductio*, and also of the relations subsisting between him and Ilacomilus. But if these relations did exist, then this pseudonymous writer could not have confounded him with Columbus, except at the Florentine's own suggestion. If, however, it was done under the orders of a superior, and without the cognizance of Vespucius; if, under these circumstances, it was proposed to impose the name of the latter upon the New Continent, then it behooved him, the intended instrument of such a wrong, to act the part of an honorable man, by elucidating the facts of the case, and rejecting such a design or even the entertainment of it. So that, considering the intimacy of the two parties, there is no doubt that the geographer was guided by the navigator in what he did.

Taking all these things into consideration, we are led to the conclusion that the name given to the New Continent, *after the death of Columbus*, was the result of a preconceived plan against his memory, either designedly and with malice aforethought, or by the secret influence of an extensive patronage of foreign merchants residing at Seville and elsewhere, dependent on Vespucius, and transacting business with him in his capacity of naval contractor, an office which he enjoyed a great many years, and which must have procured him hosts of correspondents, apologists, and flatterers.

It must here be remarked, that towards the end of the fifteenth century, as *Bossi* says, the discoveries made by the Portuguese had exalted the imaginations of all men, so that *savans*, statesmen, *merchants, as well as common sailors*, all talked of discoveries, and all aspired to add to the number of them; *likewise that there was no lack of charlatans in the cause of navigation, nor of impostors, who spread abroad their fabulous accounts to gain credit with the merchants by flattering their avarice*, and piqued the curiosity of the common people, always so greedy of novelty. They even wormed their way into courts, where they met with favor and protection. There could have been then no mystery observed in regard to discoveries, nor any great difficulty in maintaining a correspondence between Spain, Portugal, and the rest of Europe. And the great number of letters, and the many editions of them, published everywhere since 1493, prove at once the utmost facility of communication and an extensive publicity.[1]

The defenders of Vespucius say, in his justification, that he never asserted in his letters that he was the discoverer of the New Continent; but this excuse, it appears to us, falls of itself, on attentively reading his narratives. If he does not in so many words declare that it was not Columbus, but himself, who discovered it, he tries to make his readers think so by relating, in his letter of 1501, how "he reposed himself at Seville from his two voyages, which, by order of the Spanish sovereign, he made to the West Indies;" by describing the inhabitants of these countries as being of the same color as those whom he "*discovered by orders of the king of Castile;*" and by saying, "we left the port of Cadiz (which he calls Calis) the 10th of May, 1497, and in this voyage, that continued eighteen months, *we discovered a great extent of main land and an infinite number of islands!*" — a passage by which Canovai, the great panegyrist of Vespucius, would fain prove that the Florentine navigator, by his own avowal, had really discovered the continent before Columbus.[2]

[1] In the Diplomatic History of *Martin Behain*, of Nuremburg, by Murr, it can be seen, at pages 123, 124, that these communications were more easy and frequent than we are now apt to imagine them; that there were monthly deliveries of letters from Germany in Portugal, Madeira, and the Azores, and even semi-monthly by way of Antwerp and Genoa; and that too in the year 1494.

[2] See Canovai, p. 288.

We must consider that the question was the discovery of the vast continent of a New World; and a careful perusal of Vespucius's relations shows that he did all in his power to prove that the greatest part of this was owing to him. Thus we find that, when speaking of his pretended voyages made by order of the king of Portugal in 1501 and 1503,[1] he not only attributes to himself two preceding expeditions to the New World in the Spanish service, keeping a guarded silence as to Cabral's discovery of Brazil, (though this happened before his letter was written, and he could not therefore have been ignorant of it,) but, what is more, he exaggerates his discoveries, and in their false proportions proclaims them to the world.

Now, if to these false pretensions we oppose authentic documents found in the Spanish archives, and lately published, which establish the fact of Vespucius's residence at Seville till the years 1499 and 1500, whence he embarked for the *first time* with Hojeda, (a circumstance which he says nothing about, because, if he had, the expedition having been commanded by a Spaniard, and directed by Juan de la Cosa, the fame he wished to monopolize would have suffered,) if to these pretensions and concealments of the Florentine we oppose the said documents, bearing in mind what has previously been remarked by us,

[1] See the *Bulletin* of February, 1837.

it seems impossible that any one can seriously maintain that Vespucius was altogether a stranger to Ilacomilus's project, or to the designs entertained in certain countries, as to his fabulous discoveries, at the expense of Columbus, Cabral, and others. Besides, if we examine the character of Vespucius, as disclosed in his letters, there will be found, in addition to what has been already cited, expressions and entire passages which exhibit in how exaggerated a manner he set forth his pretended discoveries ; never failing, as occasion offered, to exalt himself at the cost of other navigators. Then let that portion of the dedication of the *Cosmographiæ Introductio* be called to mind, where he seizes the opportunity of boasting that he was brought up with a prince, since become king, going the length of vaunting the ties of friendship that united them. And observe, in one of his letters, when discoursing of the feigned invitation from the king of Portugal to him, with what solicitude he proclaims that he was at Seville, *reposing* himself after the fatigues he had undergone in his two preceding voyages,[1] when a messenger from the Portuguese sovereign reached him with letters patent.[2] For the purpose of giving the world a high idea of his attainments and personal importance, he wrote, on arriving at Lisbon, that *the king had expe-*

[1] The documents recently published and already cited prove the contrary.

[2] See preceding pages on this point.

*rienced great delight at seeing him*, that *the king had prayed him*, &c. &c., and *that the prayers of kings are commands*, &c. &c.

On the other hand, he treats African discoveries with a certain sort of contempt, for the sake of glorifying his own upon the New Continent, as we will show by a passage taken from the Italian text. Speaking of the expedition previously sent to the coast of Guinea by the Portuguese king, he says: "*Such a voyage as this I do not call a voyage of discovery*," &c. &c. And in the letter to Lorenzo de' Medici, in the tone of one vastly preëminent in knowledge, he asserts, "*If my memory serves me, you have some acquaintance with cosmography.*" (He makes him a simple dilettante.)

After all which has been proved by us, after the exposure we have made of the suppressions Vespucius was guilty of, and especially after the publication of his own words, wherein to a certain point are revealed his pretensions, it seems to us that we commit no injustice towards him in believing that he himself exercised a considerable influence, particularly when Columbus was dead, upon all which happened relative to imposing his name on the New World, in the hope of producing the conviction that he was the true discoverer, at least of the main land.

The recommendation of Vespucius by Columbus to his son, in a letter written at Seville the 5th of February, 1505, of which some would avail themselves to justify the Florentine, proves, on the contrary, as it appears to us, how problematical were his pretended discoveries, and how inferior he was in 1505, that is, subsequently to his four imaginary expeditions, to other maritime discoverers. For it seems evident that, if he had actually performed the four said voyages previously to 1505, such discoveries as he boasted being the author of, must have saved him from having recourse to the admiral's protection, and to a recommendation from the admiral to his son, and moreover must have been alluded to in Columbus's letter. But, so far from this being the case, Columbus confines himself to saying that "he had always been desirous of obliging him, because he had been *unfortunate*, not having gained much by his labors;" which labors were, without doubt, none other than those proved by documents in the royal Spanish archives to have been his occupation for many years, that is, the business of a ship-caterer, or of a designer of charts during his residence at Seville. By comparing Columbus's letter with the letters of Vespucius, the mass of inconsistencies contained in the latter is palpably evident; for in them he says that, "while recovering at Seville from the fatigues of his two voyages to the West Indies, he was obliged to repair to Lisbon, at the solicitation of the Portuguese sovereign, *in spite of the opposition of all that knew him*, who entreated him not to quit Spain, where *everybody so highly honored him, and the king held him in such high esteem.*" Now, how is it possible to reconcile, supposing it to be true, what he says about the favor he enjoyed in 1504 at the Spanish court, with the compassion he excited the following year in the breast of Columbus, who pitied him *because he was unfortunate?* How can the vast consideration, in which he then delighted, be accounted for, when it is seen that, after having left Spain, as he pretends, rich, and powerful on the score of discoveries he had made, he was compelled, one year later, to apply to Columbus for a recommendatory epistle to his son, because of the unhappy condition to which he was reduced? How can all this be made to correspond with the slight regard that was had for his narratives in 1515 at the council of pilots? and, in a word, how can it be made to coincide with those documents which have been lately brought to light?

It is, perhaps, on account of his expressions, his concealments and his contradictions that Vespucius is accused of having usurped the discovery of the New Continent, by so many writers and geographers, who have read his narratives without having the same means of judging them which we possess; for, in the writings, attributed to him, that have reached us, if he does not distinctly claim to be the first discoverer, he at least intimates as much with the hope of being believed. And, indeed, what interest could such a host of authors, from the time of Herrera to the present day, have had in decrying the memory of Vespucius, if they had not found in the facts related by himself, and in his own narratives, motives more or less substantial for censuring him? How can any one array himself against these authors, as Canovai has done, since it was their sagacity and research led them to discover the inconsistencies and absurdities of Vespucius's stories, and to perceive how perfectly destitute they were of the impress of truth? It cannot be said of them that they were all writers belonging to one single country who conspired against him, for a single glance at the preceding pages will suffice to show that the accounts given by this navigator, and the claims made in his behalf by panegyrists, were attacked, directly or indirectly, by authors and geographers of all countries, not excepting even the most learned and distinguished scholars in Italy.

It is argued, in Vespucius's justification, that Father Canovai, his panegyrist, successfully encountered every difficulty which presented itself in regard to the personages whom the Florentine addressed in his letters; but a simple perusal of the father's work is sufficient to show how completely he failed in his attempt. For, as has already been remarked, no one has a right to remake literary productions, as was done in the case of Vespucius's letters, for the sake of getting rid of erroneous dates and expressions, and in order to bring them into correspondence with the existences of persons to whom they were addressed, by substituting different names and dates, as did Bandini and Canovai, in the presumptuous hope of giving to such documents an authenticity and a seal of truth which originally they never had. And this is what we propose to demonstrate more in detail as we proceed, exposing, by an analysis of his work, how many offences and mistakes Canovai has committed, some of which we will immediately indicate.

## CHAPTER VI.

Wishing to explain how Vespucius could have addressed one of his letters to the duke of Lorraine, who took the title of king of Jerusalem, Canovai hazards the conjecture that probably the compilers of Vespucius's voyages, meeting frequently with the two letters V and M, read *Vostra Maèstà* instead of *Vostra Magnificenza,* — a suitable title of courtesy in respect to Soderini! But such a conjecture happens to be in direct opposition to the original text, where, written out at large, is found *Tua Majestas* and *Illustrissime Rex.*[1] By similar subtilities he strives to justify and extenuate the errors and contradictions found in the letters of Vespucius, but such means are wholly inadequate to establish the credit either of these letters or of their author.

Mr. Washington Irving[2] has with good reason refused to admit Canovai's extraordinary conjecture, for he says, this author did not reflect what inconsistency there was in treating Soderini as a sovereign prince, and adds that, " the person (Canovai) mak-

[1] See *Cosmographiæ Introductio,* 1507. We have examined this work, both M. Henry Ternaux's copy and another in the Mazarine Library.

[2] History of the Life and Voyages of Columbus, vol. iv. pp. 174, 175.

ing this remark, *can hardly have read the prologue to the Latin edition in which the title of 'your majesty' is frequently repeated,*" &c.

From this observation alone it is easy to see how pertinacious was Father Canovai in the defence of Vespucius. So prepossessed in his favor was he, that, having seen a Latin version of his letters, he asserts, without any other proof, that it was in this language they were originally written; and upon a supposition so erroneous he pronounces him to have been a *Latinist* and an eloquent writer. But, unfortunately for him, Vespucius himself gives him the most decided contradiction, by exposing his ignorance of the first rudiments of Latin, when he cites in his narrative *what Pliny wrote to Mæcenas.* For that minister, the favorite of Augustus, died eight years before the Christian era, and Pliny, the naturalist, lived under Vespasian. Titus was born thirty-one years after the death of Mæcenas, and Pliny the younger flourished subsequently to the empire of Trajan. Canovai, to justify Vespucius, would fain persuade us that he meant to say *Catullus* or *Cornelius Nepos!* Never, in our opinion, did any one ever more abuse the system of interpretation than he has done, or with more effrontery outrage both letter and spirit of the original text.

The learned Tiraboschi,[1] speaking of the literary

[1] Tiraboschi, vol. vi. pp. 1, 215.

attainments of Vespucius, in connection with what Bandini has said, thus expresses himself: "A letter, in proof of these attainments, presented by him (Bandini,) and written by Vespucius to his father, the 18th of October, 1476, when he was twenty-six years old, does not convey the most favorable impression as to the progress made by him in the higher branches of education, nor as to his elegance of style, and still less his grammatical knowledge; for he himself says, that he dares not write his letters in Latin, without having his preceptor at his side."

As to the documents produced by Canovai, we will at present confine ourselves to the remark, that he has imitated Bandini in publishing a second time the would-be new letters, found in a certain book of the Ricardian Library at Florence. But, for the better appreciating the merits of this discovery, it must be observed, that he says these letters were discovered, among others, in a small volume containing sixteen in all, without any indication either of the *year or place in which they were printed.* Yet he must have been aware of the existence of these documents through Bandini's work, who had already published one edition of it, the first that ever appeared, according to his statement, and who contented himself, at the same time, with declaring that the original of it, as it seemed to him, (*per quanto appare,*)[1] was

[1] Vita di Amerigo, p. 12.

preserved in the valuable library of the Marquis Ricardi.

We would here call attention to the jumble that has been made of these letters. Bandini presents them as never having been edited, and Canovai, without knowing any thing about it, would fain persuade us that this letter of Vespucius, newly found and unedited, as he pretends, *bore no sign of when or where it was printed.* Thus we see an already printed document brought forward by Bandini as one new and unedited, and then the same thing repeated by Canovai.

It is to be remarked of the latter that whenever he would prove the accuracy of certain texts, and their superiority over others since published, he, on the contrary, betrays his own ignorance of analysis, and his incapacity to judge of ancient documents and the characters peculiar to different epochs. What was his course as to the letters found in the Ricardian Library? He himself avows that *reasons* (which he refrains from mentioning) *decided him* to reconstruct these letters, rather than to reprint them. He collated them with the edition of Valori,[1] with Ramusio and Giuntini; but it is impossible to understand how he could speak of the edition of Baccio Valori, when that author had been dead twenty-four

[1] This is Baccio Valori, who was born in 1354, and died in 1427, and not the author of the Life of Lorenzo de' Medici, already spoken of.

years at the birth of Vespucius. So we see that one of the Florentine's panegyrists tried to foist on the world, as a novelty, a work already published, and that the other, instead of reprinting the said work, altered and remoulded it. What faith or authority, then, we ask, can be accorded to such productions, which are not even a faithful copy of what is said to have come from the Ricardian Library at Florence, and to have been found written in *ancient characters?*

Canovai has the simplicity to acknowledge that, "for the greater convenience of his readers, *he divided the letter to Soderini among the four voyages of Vespucius*, beginning with that of 1497,[1] and so going on in order." But, not content with these changes, he proceeds to the length of substituting the months of April and June for those of July and September, and then, lost in the maze of contradictions which Vespucius's two letters contain, he emerges from it only by venting his wrath on Herrera and on all those who opposed his schemes and opinions.

Navarrete has noticed the alteration in names spoken of, both in regard to persons and countries; how the same events were applied to different voyages and epochs; what various readings, by no means unimportant, were found even in the published letters and narratives; and how many were the absurdities in chronology, history, navigation,

[1] At this epoch it has been shown in the preceding pages that Vespucius was occupied in furnishing vessels with provisions.

astronomy, &c.; all of which facts induce the suspicion that these accounts are mere fabrications, in parts if not in the whole. So that, observes the erudite author, "there is no wonder that all who attempted to make themselves the historians and eulogists of Vespucius, have been misled and bewildered by deviating from the path of truth," &c.

This occupation of Canovai, the alteration and mutilation of original documents, which is admissible on no account whatever, was attacked at Florence the moment that the results of it appeared, as is revealed to us by two little pamphlets which were published, one entitled, *Annotazioni sincere dell' Autore dell' Elogio premiato di Amerigo Vespucci, per una seconda edizione;* and the other, *Lettera allo Stampatore Sig. Pietro Allegrini a nome dell' Autore dell' Elogio premiato di Amerigo Vespucci,* the 25th of February, 1789.[1] It is in the latter of these, especially, that Canovai exhibits an unbridled rage against his adversaries, and particularly against those persons who *idled away their time inhaling the fresh air upon the piazza of Santa Croce,* while he was engaged in devouring the Cosmography of Sebastian Munster!

These two pamphlets are not the only productions which shed much light upon the discussions that

[1] The refutation of this pamphlet of Canovai's by Bartolozzi, who powerfully contested its truth, is very curious. See *Apologia delle Ricerche Istorico-critiche,* Florence, 1789.

arose, even in Florence, out of Canovai's panegyric: there are others we will cite, as they are but little known, and we think this will be of the greater service, because of their making part of the materials which relate to the work of Canovai.

Seven years after the appearance of this work, so slight progress had it made in converting the incredulous, that, besides the two pamphlets just spoken of, an anonymous writer, assuming the name of Diophantus, the Greek mathematician of Alexandria, but whom we believe to have been Canovai himself, published another under the title of *Difesa di Amerigo Vespucio.* It is in duodecimo, contains fifteen pages, and bears the date of February 29th, 1796. It is in the form of a letter addressed to the author of *Reflections upon the Panegyric of Machiavel*, a work dedicated to Muñoz, and printed the preceding year (1795) at Cesena, in which Vespucius is regarded as an impostor, notwithstanding Canovai's famous eulogy upon him. As the defence of Vespucius is not touched upon in the first six pages of this production, it can be found, if anywhere, only in the nine remaining ones. But though there is really nothing worthy of an analysis in the whole, it, nevertheless, furnishes an additional proof of the literary war which broke out at Florence, in the years 1788 and 1789, on the subject of the eulogy upon Vespucius. Yet, beyond this, it is remarkable on no account, except for the confusion which pervades it throughout, and for a complete absence of all proofs that might put an end to the uncertainty resting upon the truth of Vespucius's narratives.

A clever and vigorous refutation of Canovai appeared at Florence in 1789, under the title of *Ricerche Istorico-critiche*, &c., in which the author, Bartolozzi, at page 7, says that Canovai added to his eulogy on Americus Vespucius a justificatory dissertation, wherein, for the purpose of defending that celebrated navigator, he greatly disguised the truth of history. Also that there was published against this production, with the title of *Annotazioni Sincere*, a pamphlet, to which a reply still more indecent was made, having for its title *Lettera allo Stampatore*. "I would gladly pass in silence," he continues, "these two contemptible pamphlets, which are a disgrace to literature, and the second of which finds no excuse in either the education or literary merit of its author, who did not blush to put his name to it." In a word, Bartolozzi devotes his fourteenth chapter to a refutation of Canovai's work, which we shall revert to again hereafter. At present, we would in passing mention another circumstance, not less singular, touching what passed at Florence respecting the prize, which the few partisans of Canovai, quitting the subject of Vespucius, have made use of as an argument in favor of the Florentine, without assigning any other reason but that *it was awarded to the said Eulogy of Canovai's.*

Those persons who believe that the prize founded by the Count of Durfort was instituted in favor of the best panegyric upon Vespucius, are completely mistaken; for the letters addressed by that diplomatist to the Academy of Cortona, dated the 24th and 28th of September, 1787, show that he attached no importance whatever to such a subject. It was, on the contrary, considerations of a later date, and quite foreign to the original intentions of the founder, which decided the Academy to add the eulogy upon Vespucius to what had already been proposed as a theme by M. Durfort. And in its programme the Academy itself, in honor of Columbus, speaking of Vespucius, says, — "*whom after the glorious deeds of the celebrated Columbus*," etc.[1] So that this learned Academy paid the highest compliment possible to Columbus, while Canovai was exerting himself in every way to persuade the world that Vespucius was the discoverer of the New Continent. Canovai's design is betrayed from the very commencement of his work upon the life of the Florentine navigator; he indicates passages in certain authors who pretend that America was known before the time of Columbus; he does not forget even Cabot, saying that he above all others could most impair the glory of Columbus, not reflecting that by so doing he equally tarnished the false fame of Ves-

1 Monumenti relativi al giudizio pronunziato dall' Accademia Etrusca di Cortona di un Elogio di Amerigo Vespuccio. Arezzo, 1787.

pucius, whom he wished to exalt at the expense of that great man. In spite, however, of these citations, his show of profound erudition is by no means great; for he forgot to quote Erasmus Schmid,[1] who pretended that Homer had known America; also Adam of Bremen and Cassel, in his historical observations, *De Navigatione fortuita in Americam sæculo XI. facta;*[2] likewise, Gottlob Fritsch, in a work called, *Disputatio Historico-geographica in qua quæritur utrum veteres Americam noverint nec-ne;* and, in a word, he has forgotten the productions of Daniel Victor,[3] of Torfæus,[4] of De Guines,[5] and of Scherer.[6] But, let this be as it may, if Columbus thought, in common with Aristotle, Marinus of Tyre and other old authors, that the nearest points of India were not very distant from Spain, we again say that this fortunate error respecting the dimensions of the globe, which was the moving cause of Columbus's enterprise, proves that he was wiser than the enemies of his fame believed him to be.[7]

Canovai, who in spite of himself passes an enco-

[1] Fabricius, Bibliotheca Græca, vol. i. p. 345.

[2] Magdeburg, 1741.

[3] Jena, 1670. 8vo.

[4] Hafniæ (*Copenhagen*,) 1705. 8vo. 1715.

[5] Remarques Géopraphiques et Critiques, etc. This author pretends that the Chinese had established a flourishing commerce in South America, in the 458th year of our Lord.

[6] Recherches Historiques et Géographiques sur le Nouveau Monde. Paris, 1777.

[7] See Malte-Brun.

mium on Columbus in another place,[1] manifests the greatest reserve as to all which concerns the discovery of the main land, in order to bestow the glory of that on Vespucius. Indeed, at page 182, throwing off all disguise, he says: "*Here, it is true, the daring Columbus ought to have arrived the first, if he intended to take from everybody else the hope of excelling him. But every such attempt is vain, and whoever regarded the discovery of the Continent as only a poor appendix to that of the islands, was guilty of making war upon truth itself, without offending by such means the invulnerable glory of Americus.*" And elsewhere the author exhibits yet more plainly his hostile sentiments towards Columbus, when speaking of Vespucius: "*Just as if,*" he remarks, "*the humiliating repulses Columbus encountered, his jealousy, mishaps, and mercantile greediness had been concealed from the intelligent navigator.*"[2]

This panegyrist of Vespucius expresses his surprise at finding the enemies and adversaries of the Florentine to be men of celebrity and importance; and he appears to be especially astonished to see ranking among them the learned Tiraboschi, in whose work he says is found every thing ever written against Vespucius,[3] an assertion which speaks very little for the erudition of Canovai. Nevertheless, he

1 Canovai, p. 170, posthumous edition of 1817.

2 Ibid. p. 264.

3 Canovai, pp. 170, 212.

has seen fit to reply to Tiraboschi, notwithstanding the extreme moderation of that author, who, so far from attacking Americus, as it is pretended, rather sought for motives in his justification, scarcely accusing him of want of sincerity in his narratives, wherein the names of Hojeda and Juan de la Cosa are suppressed, and none of the ports of landing are designated.

The manner in which Canovai attempts to vindicate Vespucius from Tiraboschi's accusation, is exceedingly convenient, but, at the same time, very unsafe. He asserts that the Florentine navigator never accompanied Hojeda! and gives as a proof of his assertion an inference drawn from the difference of character, interest, and morality in these two men, — a difference which must have rendered impossible a union between a savant (Vespucius) and an ignorant soldier (Hojeda.) In a word, he advisedly calls Tiraboschi an eternal copyist of every lie! But, unhappily for him, authentic documents prove quite the contrary of what he advances. They establish, beyond a doubt, that it was with Hojeda and Juan de la Cosa that Vespucius made the only voyage which is not problematical, the only one which is not a matter of doubtful discussion.[1] And in demonstrating the falseness of Canovai's hypothesis, they overthrow all the arguments by which this

[1] See the documents of Seville and of Simancas in Navarrete, vol. iii., and preceding pages of this work.

author endeavors to support his erroneous assertion, destroying at the same time the entire foundation of his justificatory dissertation.

Bartolozzi himself, though unacquainted with the documents lately published, remarks, in a part of his work, upon Canovai's folly for having attacked Tiraboschi respecting another point, whereupon the latter made no mistake ; but, in correcting which imaginary error, the former fell into a very serious one, leading him, as it did, into a great number of others, that would have been avoided, had he properly studied the geographical question before casting censure upon the author of the *History of Italian Literature.* Canovai makes use of a singular expedient in the fabrication of Vespucius's eulogium, and at the expense of all those who preceded that navigator. He seems to reprimand them for the purpose of exalting him ; to accomplish which he spares neither contumelious language of the grossest nature, nor assertions absurd to the last degree.

It will be well to give some few instances of the latter. If the object be to make us believe that Vespucius passed the equinoctial line, he says, *the selfsame Vespucius stood astonished at his own magnanimous daring!* But he forgets the daring of the Portuguese that went before the Florentine, (who was at that time in Italy,) and in 1471 discovered Annaboa, and Congo in 1484. He forgets Bartholomew Dias, the discoverer of the *Cabo Tor-*

*mentoso* in 1486, and would fain convince us that Vespucius was the first to pass the equator. In another place he tells us that Cabral, had not the fame of the Florentine's discovery reached him, would never have ventured, in his expedition, to rush from east to west, as he did. In a word, he does not even remember the documents of Ramusio.[1] Then, after declaring that Pinzon and Lepe visited the western continent, following the steps of the *invincible navigator*, he assures us in another place that the discovery of Brazil was one altogether accidental![2] The celebrated Cook, according to him, repeated nothing but what *Vespucius had a long time before observed and decided upon!*[3] And the name of America was solely a brilliant recompense awarded to the Florentine by Ferdinand the Catholic, who ordained by *letters patent* that the New Continent should be called by his name, thereby honoring both him and the New World! To which account he adds, "the *simplicity of the thought* has been so agreeable to Europe, that the royal grace accorded became almost a law for that entire portion of the world." But, although every one well read in the history of discoveries, and in that of Spain, is aware of the falseness of all this, that the appellation of America is never found in the principal historians

[1] The letter of Pedro Vaz Caminha alone, without the entire history, suffices to overthrow the author's assertions.

[2] Canovai, p. 133.

[3] Ibid. p. 150, note 147.

of Spain, and that the Spaniards never gave to the New Continent any name except that of the Western Indies, yet Canovai, regardless of all this, braves every thing for the sake of gaining credit for his own story.

If the pretended letters patent had ever been promulgated, would Peter Martyr have named his history *De Orbe Novo*, (a work published at Alcala in 1516,) or, if the ordinance spoken of had ever existed, would Enciso have, in 1519, entitled his production *Summa Geographia de las Indias?* Would the letters of Ferdinand Cortès, printed at Seville in 1522 and 1523, in the case supposed, have applied any other name than that of America to these territories; or, would have Oviedo called his history, *Historia General y Natural de las Indias?* Such an ordinance having been made, why is it not to be found in the Collection of the Laws of the Indies, published at Alcala in 1543, not under the title of Laws upon *America*, but *Leyes y Ordonnança para la Governacion de las Indias?* Facts like these, then, and documents lately published, completely nullify the assertion of Canovai.

Is it not evident that, if letters patent from king Ferdinand, like those described, had ever been accorded to Vespucius, the Spaniards would have called the New Continent after his name ? And is it not evident, too, that if such decision in council as the one pretended, had ever taken place, Vespucius would not have stood in need of Columbus's recommendation in 1505, *on account of his being unfortunate?* Then again, would not that great navigator himself have opposed any concession of the sort to the Florentine, instead of recommending to his own son a man who had been capable of committing an act of such usurpation and wrong against his own person?

But if Canovai has taken for granted the said fictitious letters patent, which imposed the name of America on the New Continent, he elsewhere, and with an additional contradiction, betrays his ignorance of the ancient charts of this portion of the world. If these, he says, were well examined, and likewise the old historians of the New Continent, it would be found that the name of America was not at first given to the entire continent, but only to Brazil,[1] when, as we can affirm from personal inspection, the ancient charts themselves prove quite the contrary. Thus, in that of the New Continent designed by *Juan de la Cosa* at Puerto de Santa Maria, in 1500, the original of which is in the possession of our learned fellow-laborer, M. Walckenaer, no designation whatever is given to the southern part. In an outline traced by this *savant* are to be remarked two islands, which, by their position, appear, both in his opinion and our own, to be the isle of Ferdinand de Noronha, and a number of small islets greatly exag-

[1] Canovai, Elogio di Vespucci, p. 346.

gerated. Beside one of them is seen the flag of Portugal, with this note: — *Islas descubiertas por el Rey de Portugal;* and north of the position of Cape Saint Augustine, are these words: — *Este Cabo se descubriò en año de* 1499, *por Castilla, siendo descubridor Vicentians.*[1]

Another argument still does this contemporary document present in opposition to the pretended discoveries of Vespucius, inasmuch as its author takes not the slightest notice of them, and yet he was the companion of Columbus in his second voyage, and of Hojeda and Vespucius in their expedition of 1499–1500. Juan de la Cosa was so skilful that he esteemed himself superior in nautical knowledge even to Columbus,[2] and in all which concerned discoveries he was such an adept that every thing new immediately found a place in his map.[3] Is it probable then, that he, who affixed to one point of the coast the

[1] This precious geographical monument is drawn upon a parchment more than fifteen feet square. It comprises not only America, but also Europe, Asia, and Africa. M. de Humboldt's *Examen Critique* contains a part of it, which he caused to be engraved. M. de la Sagra also has done the same with regard to another large portion of this World-Map, comprising the New Continent, for the purpose of illustrating his important work, *Histoire Physique, Politique et Naturelle de l'Ile de Cuba*, printed at Paris in 1837.

[2] This is that Juan de la Cosa, says M. de Humboldt, in his *Examen Critique*, etc., of whom, according to the testimony of Bernardo de Ibarra, in the suit of the Treasury against Don Diego Columbus, the Admiral complains, because he, Cosa, a clever man, pretended to know more than he.

[3] See observation of M. de la Sagra, *Histoire de l'Ile de Cuba*, p. 5.

name of its discoverer, would have failed to attach the name of Vespucius, his fellow-voyager, to another, if, indeed, any part of the New Continent had been discovered by the Florentine? The note, too, inscribed beside the island of Ferdinand de Noronha, upon the map we are speaking of, does it not show that the Portuguese had already effected the other discovery, without the intervention of Vespucius, whom Cosa, his companion, would certainly have mentioned by name, if he had discovered a single point of the New Continent for the king of Portugal, and much more if he had been the first who found out the whole Southern Continent.

But, however this may be, in continuing to demonstrate how Canovai deceived himself through ignorance of the ancient charts, we will add, that in the map of the world by Ruysch, in the edition of Ptolemy, published at Rome in 1508, the southern part of the New Continent is represented under the name of, The Land of the Holy Cross, or The New World, (*Terra Sanctæ-Crucis, sive Mundus-Novus,*) and in the position of Cape Saint Augustine, we read: "The Cape of the Holy Cross," (*Caput Sanctæ-Crucis*); — that in a map of the world, contained in the edition of Ptolemy, by *Bernardus Sylvanus Eboliensis*, published at Venice in 1511,[1] is seen the southern part of the New Continent under the name

[1] Copy in the Royal Library.

of *Terra Sanctæ-Crucis ;* — that in a chart found in the first edition of Peter Martyr (1511) no designation is met with on the same portion of the said continent but that of *Caput Sanctæ-Crucis,* which is applied to Saint Augustine ;[1] and lastly, that in a beautiful edition of Ptolemy, published at Strasburg in 1513, by Johannes Scottus, there is a map of the New Continent, in the southern part of which only, the same cape is marked with the same name. The coast therein is laid down as far as the fortieth degree of south latitude, and in another map, bearing the title of *Terræ Novæ,* by the side of Paria is the following note, in Latin: — "*This land, and the adjacent islands, were discovered by Columbus, a Genoese, acting under the orders of the king of Castile.*"

In a preface which precedes the new maps, it is said that the *marine chart,* called *the Admiral's,* had been first drawn according to the orders of Ferdinand the Catholic, (erroneously termed king of Portugal,)[2] and corrected and enlarged by means of contributions from celebrated navigators, and published as a testimony to the liberality of René of Lorraine.

Now, let it be remarked here, that all these particulars are very curious, and of vast importance in

[1] Library of M. Ternaux.

[2] In the text it is *Serenissimi Portugalliæ regis Ferdinandi,* — an evident error, for the King Ferdinand of Portugal died the 22d of October, 1383, one hundred and ten years before the discovery of the New Continent.

a discussion like the present. The marine chart, we see, was called the *Chart of the Admiral*, and it was therefore originally designed either by Columbus or Cabral, but never by Vespucius, for he attained to no such rank as that of admiral. There is no doubt, however, that, if it was not the immediate work of Columbus, it was done either by his orders or subsequently to his discoveries. And it is a fact that he sent to the Catholic sovereigns a marine chart of the New Continent, together with a letter, in which he makes mention of it.[1] A copy of this chart, which doubtless already marked the main land, Hojeda made use of in pursuing the same route as he had done;[2] as can easily be ascertained by inspecting the depositions contained in the suit against Columbus, where Hojeda testifies that he *saw the chart sent by the Admiral to the King and Queen at Castile.*[3] In the same law process is to be observed the answer of Bernardo de Ibarra, who confirms the fact that the *chart of the Admiral* was sent to the Catholic sovereigns; and he adds, that he had heard of others having been made after it, which Merino, Hojeda, and other persons availed themselves of in prosecuting their voyages to these latitudes.[4]

It appears, then, an indisputable matter: 1, that

[1] See Navarrete, vol. i. pp. 253, 264, and La Sagra's *Histoire de l'Ile de Cuba.*

[2] Ibid. vol. i. p. 5.

[3] Ibid. vol. iii. p. 539.

[4] Ibid. p. 587.

the earliest charts of the New Continent were designed by Columbus, or by his directions, and moreover that he preceded Vespucius in this work. Indeed, we see in a letter of Angelo Trivigiano to Malapiero, already cited by us, that, referring to a map of Columbus's voyage, which was required of him, (probably by the Venetian government, as Bossi thinks,) he replies: 1. *There is none here* (in Grenada) *with the single exception of Columbus's own, nor is there anybody capable of designing one:*[1] — 2. that the marine chart called *the Admiral's*, which had been drawn and corrected according to the commands of King Ferdinand, and engraved by the care of René of Lorraine, which is treated of, too, in the preface to this edition of Ptolemy, was probably one of those copies spoken of by Ibarra; and 3. that what is found in the said preface, to wit, how the chart in question was made according to the orders of Ferdinand the Catholic, and published with additions through the care of René of Lorraine, joined to the testimony of documents which we have quoted, demonstrates still more strongly, that the relations subsisting between René and Spain respecting these geographical questions, establish the fact of the Admiral's discoveries, so that neither the duke nor Ilacomilus could have been ignorant of them, or have

[1] The Queen Isabella, in a letter to Columbus, dated September 5, 1493, speaks of the marine chart he had designed, and asks it of him. See Navarrete, vol. ii. document 10.

attributed them to Vespucius, without being guilty of a flagrant injustice.

Again, one continues to find, as for example in the map called *Orbis Typus Universalis*, that the southern part of the New Continent is not denominated America, and even that the name of *Sanctæ Crucis*, originally given by Cabral, is invariably employed to designate it. And, besides this curious fact, we will point out another, which is, that *Philesius*, that is, Professor Ringmann of Bâle, the correspondent of Ilacomilus, took no small share in that publication, wherein the Admiral Columbus is declared to have been the first discoverer of the New Continent, and in which the southern portion of it bears no other name but that it received from Cabral. This is shown by the words of the text, as follows: *Philesii diligentiam in hoc plurimum coöperatam scias, cujus fideli doctaque manu totum quod vides opus transcriptum*, etc.[1]

We have already spoken of a map of the world called *Orbis Typus Universalis*, wherein no name is found upon the New Southern Continent, except that of "Cape of the Holy Cross," (*Caput Sanctæ Crucis*,) which is assigned to Cape Saint Augustine; and we have alluded to another chart, bearing the title of *Tabula Terræ Novæ*, in which, by the side of Paria is the following note (in Latin): "*This*

[1] The vindication of this edition of Ptolemy may be seen in Raidel's *Commentatio critico-literaria de Claudii Ptolemæi Geographia.*

*land and the adjacent islands were discovered by Columbus, a Genoese, acting under the orders of the king of Castile.*" In the latter all the coasts are laid down with their names, and on the Brazilian coasts the names are in the Portugüese language, with one single exception, that of *Caput Sanctæ Crucis*, applied to Cape Saint Augustine. Thus, then, according to an examination of those maps of the New Continent, which can be termed ancient, that is, from the publication of the earliest of them till the appearance of a world-map of Apian in 1520,[1] (in which the name of America is seen for the first time,) just the reverse of Canovai's hypothesis is found to be the fact, and *the denomination originally affixed by Cabral was constantly preserved.* The note too attached to Paria confirms Columbus's discovery, without the slightest question being raised as to Vespucius or the name of America in any of the maps abovementioned. Nevertheless these maps ought not to be regarded as the only ancient ones, according to Canovai's expression, but all should likewise be included in the category which preceded the translation of the *Cosmographia* of Munster (1550) ; for the said work is his point of departure in the course of his reasoning. Consequently we shall cite other maps which can be classed as ancient, and which offer new proofs of what has already been demonstrated.

[1] In the *Solinus* of Camers.

In the *Isolario* of Bordone, printed at Venice in 1528, a chart of the southern part of the New Continent is found, with the following note (in Italian): "*Part of the territory of the New World*, and the text says, that *these islands were discovered by the Spaniards and Portuguese.* At page 10, the southern portion being mentioned, it is called by the name which Cabral gave it, *The Land of the Holy Cross, or The New World.*[1] In a second edition of the same work, printed also at Venice, in 1533, there is a map of the world wherein the southern part of the New Continent is designated as the New World, and likewise another, but of the preceding year (1532,) in which the name of *The Land of the Holy Cross, or, New World*, is given to it.[2] In a later edition too, that of 1547, we meet with the same appellation applied to the same territory.[3]

And here it will be permitted us to make an observation, seriously affecting this discussion, which is, that the authority of Bordoni's work is of the greater importance, because the denominations contained in his text and charts give additional weight to the testimony hitherto advanced by us in opposition to the pretensions of Vespucius's eulogists; for Bordoni was the contemporary of Vespucius,[4] was an

[1] Copy in the Library of the Institute.

[2] Edition in the Royal Library.

[3] For this edition we are indebted to our learned fellow-laborer, M. Jomard.

[4] Bordoni was born in the fifteenth century, and died in 1531.

Italian, was deeply read in geography, voyages, and discoveries, and by the book in question acquired greater renown than by his collection of Latin translations of Lucian's Dialogues, or by his *Description of Italy.*

In the edition of Mola by Vadianus of Bâle,[1] there is a chart dated 1520, wherein, upon the southern portion of the New Continent, is this note (in Latin): *This land and the neighboring islands were discovered, in* 1497, *by Columbus, a Genoese, acting by orders of the king of Castile.* In another edition of 1540, the position of Saint Augustine is marked by the words, *Caput Sanctæ Crucis;* and in yet another, of 1572, published at Paris, is found a map of the New World, with *Novus Orbis* attached to the southern quarter, and, besides the designation of *America, sive, Novi Orbis Pars,* in the Portuguese part the word *Brasilia* is seen.

In a chart which was engraved about the year 1562, the south part of the New Continent is designated by *Peruviana.*[2] In another, engraved towards the year 1565, by Paulo Forlani, a Veronese, the New Continent appears without the name America;[3] and on a very badly translated map of the world in an atlas dated 1567, the charts of which are drawn and illuminated on vellum, it does not go

[1] Library of M. Jomard.

[2] Department of Geographical Charts at the Royal Library.

[3] Ibid.

by that name, while the Portuguese portion is termed Brazil.[1]

It appears then, according to what we have shown, how great are the errors, concerning the ancient maps of the New Continent, into which Canovai fell. Equally apparent, too, is it that he never examined these maps. We will next, therefore, proceed to the exposure of another mistake of the panegyrist of the Florentine, who affirms, that in almost all of the editions of Ptolemy, published from 1511 to 1590, we find the map "*delle Nuove Terre col Brasile chiamato America.*"[2]

Now, this assertion of father Canovai is just as inexact as what he before says, which is proved by no less than twenty-five editions of Ptolemy, that we have consulted, from 1511 to 1584.[3] Of these,

[1] In the library of M. Ternaux.

[2] Elogio, p. 347.

[3] We will in this note briefly indicate the chronological series of these editions, beginning with that of,

1511. Ptolemy of *Bernardus Sylvanus.*
1513. Strasburg edition, by *Scottus.*
1514. Nuremburg do., (without maps.)
1520. ————, (without maps.)
1523. Ptolemy, in which, for the first time, the name of America is found upon a map.
1524. Nuremburg edition.
1527. Paris do.
1528. Venice do.
1533. ———, with a Greek text preceded by a preface of Erasmus, (without maps.)
1535. Edition of Bilibaldus Pirckeymerus.
1538. Bâle edition, in folio.
1540. Cologne do., 12mo., (without maps.)

some have a Greek text without geographical charts, and others have simply maps of the world, such as it was understood to be in the time of the great geographer, while others, and by far the greatest number, contain new maps. And it is these last, as we have already said, which disprove the assertion of Canovai. Such, for example, besides those cited by us above, is the edition published at Venice, in 8vo., by Mattiolo, in 1548. In one of its maps the New Southern Continent is indicated by the title of *Terra Nova*, and in the Portuguese part of it is found only *Brazil* written. In the two other maps where the New World appears, the same designation of *Terra Nova* is given to the southern portion. And in the Ptolemy of Ruscelli, of 1561, this portion of territory is again called by the same name, as it is also in that of Malombra, of 1575. Thus, then, as we have remarked, twenty-five editions of Ptolemy prove directly the reverse of Canovai's words.

Now let us examine those editions, in the maps of

1541. Edition of Villanovanus [Servetus.]
1545. " (another.)
1546. Paris edition in 4to., Greek text, (without maps.)
1548. Italian translation by Mattiolo, in 8vo., (with maps.)
1552. Bâle edition, (with maps.)
1559. Ptolemy, (without maps.)
1561. " by Ruscelli, (Venice.)
1568. Another Venice edition.
1574. Another edition.
1575. Venice edition, (with maps.)
1582. Bâle do.
1585. Edition of Mercator.

which the name *America* is applied to the New Continent, that is, those of 1522, 1541, and 1552 ; and we wish it to be observed at once, that even these maps themselves are not entirely favorable to the panegyrists of Vespucius. In the Ptolemy of 1541, by Villanovanus, the New Continent is indicated in the *Tabula Terræ Novæ*, and Columbus is there pointed out as the first discoverer of *Terra Firma*. There, too, is found alongside of *Paria* the note already twice quoted : *This land and the adjacent islands*, &c. &c., and in the centre is written, *Terra Nova*. And the only note in which there is any mention of Vespucius is as follows: "*Those who contend that this continent should be called America, are altogether in the wrong, since Americus did not visit it till long after Columbus.*"

In the edition of 1552, printed at Bâle, the southern part of the continent is called America, but this name is accompanied by several others ; so that the 26th map shows us what confusion and uncertainty existed respecting it. We there read, on the southern part, *Insula Atlantica, quam vocant Brazilii et Americam!* There can be no doubt, then, after what we have said, how perfectly inaccurate are the assertions of Canovai, who never studied, and was profoundly ignorant of the old maps.

The famous map of the world, in the *Solinus* of Camers, (1520,) presents, it is true, upon its title-page what follows : *Typus Orbis universalis, juxta*

*Ptolmeœi Cosmographi traditionem, et Americi Vesputii, aliorumque, Lustrationes, a Petri Appiano elaborata. A. D.* 1520 ; — but then, the note to the map of the *southern part* is altogether adverse to Canovai's exclusive assertions, and to the pretensions of Vespucius's eulogists. "*In the year* 1497," it says, "*this land and the adjacent islands were discovered by Columbus,*" etc. etc. ; and lower down is found, *America Provincia.*

In the maps of the several editions of Munster's *Cosmography*, nothing is met with of so favorable a nature for the fictitious claims of Canovai as he would fain make us suppose ; for in them there is no one denomination applied to the New Continent, decidedly fixed and uniform. In the map of the world in the German edition of 1544, the southern part of the said continent is called America, *sive Insula Brazilii ;* and in another we find, *Insula Atlantica, quam vocant Brazilii et Americam ;* and the same denomination presents itself in yet another, belonging to the edition of 1552, which has the title of *A List of New Islands.* In a map of the world which is contained in the *Cosmographia* of Hieronymo Girava, of Tarragona, published at Milan, the 18th of April, 1556,[1] the Continent is without the name of America. On the northern portion, the words *Nueva España* alone are found, and on the southern,

[1] Library of M. Ternaux. [There is a copy of this edition in the Library of Harvard College.]

*Peru*, *Chile*, and *Brasil*. This map was drawn after another by Gaspard Vopelio, of Magdeburg, dated 1547, which, in the opinion of Girava, exceeded in correctness all that had preceded it. But, however the case may be, the author of this *Cosmography*, who was better versed in ancient and modern authorities than the pseudonymous *Ilacomilus*, (the author of the celebrated *Cosmographiæ Introductio* of 1507,) says nothing whatever of the fabulous discoveries of Vespucius, nor of his astronomical observations. He remarks, that the appellation most generally given to the new continent was *Indies*, or *New World;* and, in fact, that division of his work which is devoted to this portion of the globe bears these two titles. "All the land lately discovered," says he, "is called *India*, because Christopher Columbus, a famous navigator though an ordinary cosmographer, when he obtained permission, in 1492, to search for unknown territories, named them the *Indies* on their discovery; whence, since that time, this *Terra Firma* has been always denominated *India*." And, too, it should be noted, that the cosmographer now spoken of, in mentioning the names of the earliest discoverers of the new continent, such as Columbus, the Pinzons, etc. etc. as also the Spanish writers and travellers who preceded the discovery, *Oviedo*, for example, Gomara, Ceiça, Valboâ, *Orellana*, Solis, and others, does not allude in any manner to Vespucius, whose pretensions could not have been unknown to him, since his work was composed at Milan; he had visited Germany, he had made use of the productions of Henricus Glareanus, of the *Cosmographia* of Munster, and was likewise intimately familiar with the publications of the celebrated Dutch cosmographer *Gemma Frisio*, the editor of an edition of the *Cosmographia* of Apian, (1529,) in which Vespucius is indicated as the discoverer of the new continent in 1497!!

The arguments here adduced, negative as they may appear to some, are nevertheless of immense importance, and especially when it is remembered that Girava, whom a learned contemporary calls *a man of great genius and distinguished erudition*, notwithstanding he was thoroughly acquainted with the letters of Vespucius, and every thing respecting them published by his predecessors, carefully abstains from repeating these errors, and withholds all belief from the pretended discoveries of the Florentine.

In the *Cosmography* of Belleforest, (1575,) and in the map of the New World which it contains, the northern portion is called *America, sive India Nova*, with this note attached,—*Discovered in the year* 1492, *by Christopher Columbus, in the name of the king of Castile*, while in the southern portion the name of America is not found, but only that of Brazil. Again, in the map of the world published by the learned Ortelius, (1570,) in his *Theatrum Orbis Terrarum*, the northern part of the new continent is called *America, sive India Nova*; but not so the southern, where the Portuguese possessions bear the name of Brazil. The map itself, however, of the continent, belonging to this work, has no denomination whatever; and only upon the Portuguese possessions are seen these words, *Brazilia, a Lusitanis anno* 1504 *inventa:* a date not exact, as it ought to be 1500. Moreover, the opinion of the erudite geographer is not favorable to the claims made by the panegyrists of Vespucius on his behalf. But we will confine ourselves to the citation of the following passage: — "It seems to surpass the bounds of human admiration, that this entire hemisphere, now called America, and on account of its immense extent the New World, should have remained unknown to the ancients till 1492, when it was discovered by Christopher Columbus, a Genoese."

In the *Cosmographie* of Thevet, printed at Paris in 1575, there is a map of the new continent without any designation applied to the Northern part but that of *Terre-Neuve;* and in the maps of another edition of Ortelius, (1584,) the southern portion is *not* called *America*. In the *Miroir du Monde*, too, published at Antwerp in 1584, there is a map of the said continent, engraved in 1574, wherein the name of America does not appear, but, on the contrary, a note which establishes the priority of Columbus's discovery in 1492. In a work, also, entitled *Les Trois Mondes*, by M. de la Popellinière, printed at Paris in 1582, a map of the world is found in which the northern part is designated under the name of America, and yet with this note accompanying it: — "*America, or New India, discovered in* 1492, *by Christopher Columbus, in the name of the king of Castile.*"[1]

In a German [Dutch] book called, *Conqueste van Indien*, etc. printed at Amsterdam in 1596,[2] we meet with a map in which *Peruana*, and not America, marks the southern part of the continent; and in another German [Dutch] work, entitled *Spieghel*, etc. (a translation of the Mirror of Tyranny, by Las Casas,) and likewise printed at Amsterdam in the same year, (1596,)[3] it is on the northern portion alone that the name of America is found, with these words, — *America, an.* 1492 *a Christoph. Columbo inventa;* but on the southern we read, *Caribana & Brazil.* There is also in the German translation of Leo Africanus,[4] a map of the new south continent bearing the sole designation of *Peruana.*

The following facts, then, it seems to us, may be deduced from this long examination of a great number of ancient charts: —

1. The priority of discovery by Columbus of the new continent, that is, the Terra Firma, is decided without contradiction and without exception, by all the geographical maps up to the year 1520.

2. During the same period, the southern part of

[1] Library of M. Ternaux. [2] Ibid. [3] Ibid. [4] Ibid.

the said continent, and especially Brazil, is by the same documents called The Land of the Holy Cross, (*Terra Sanctæ Crucis,*) a name originally given by the Portuguese Admiral Cabral;[1] which, together with the preceding statement, is confirmed by the maps of the sixteenth century, and more generally accepted than other denominations, which a judicious criticism refuses to acknowledge; for the discoveries of Columbus and Cabral were incontestable, while the Platonic title of *Insula Atlantica,* in the Munster charts, and of *Insula Brasilica,* were nothing

[1] In the third volume of *Memoirs Relating to the History of Nations beyond the Sea*, published by the Royal Academy of Sciences at Lisbon, there is a long notice upon Brazil, more important, in our opinion, than that of Magalhaes Gandavo, it having been written at the time when the *History of the Province of Santa Cruz* was composed by Magalhaes. It was dedicated to Don Christovao de Moura, Counsellor of State, in 1589, and its author had resided in Brazil seventeen years. Like Gandavo, he devotes his first chapter to the discovery of this part of the New World, which he says was made by Cabral, the 25th of April, 1500, and that this vast country was for several years called the province of *Santa Cruz.* Without one word of Vespucius, he declares that, after Cabral, Gonçalo Coelho was sent there with three caravels, to explore the coasts, that during several months he was thus occupied, seeking for harbors and running lines of demarcation, and that he encountered great hardships, incurring many risks, on account of the little experience and knowledge then possessed as to the direction of the coasts, and the prevailing winds. Now, it is altogether incredible that the pretended discoveries of Vespucius, and his verifications were then unknown to the author, who devoted a portion of his life to the study of this country and of its discovery, and who, living at the time of Coelho, must have seen the work of this captain and the account of his voyage; for he, of all the historians of the sixteenth century, gives the most accurate ideas respecting this voyage.

but a continuation of geographical errors proceeding from the earliest and middle ages, the name of America being a pure usurpation.

3. After the map in the *Solin* of Camers, (1520,) the name of America, which there for the first time appears, as applied to the new continent, is never encountered in any charts, in the character of a denomination indisputably fixed and generally admitted in chartography. For, even where it is met with, it is invariably seen in relation with some other, such as *Atlantic Island*, or *Brasilia*, *New Land*, *Peruviana*, *New India*, etc.; and almost constantly it is accompanied in all these same maps, even without excepting that of *Solin*, by a note which indicates Columbus as the first discoverer of the new continent.

Such has been the prodigious contest between truth and usurpation, and such has been the hesitation of those who, sometimes through partiality, but more often through ignorance, have labored to rob the great navigator of the immortal glory which belongs to his name.[1]

[1] We find, too, a continuation of this contest in a great many charts of the seventeenth century, a few examples of which we will give. In a German work called *West und ostindischer Lustgart*, &c. (The Garden of pleasure in the East and West Indies,) published at Stuttgart, [Cologne ?] in 1618, there is a map of the New World, in which the northern part alone is indicated by the name of America. And the same is true of another map, in the edition of Ortellius, of 1624, published at Antwerp; while in the southern part is this singular note: *Ophir, Montano, Postelo et Goropio!*

In a Spanish translation of Pliny, by Huerta, printed in 1625, the frontispiece contains a map of the new continent, in which the north is called *Nueva España*, and the south, simply *Peru*. And in a map of the world attached to the work, the same appellations are repeated, only to the name of Peru is added that of Brasil.

In the narrative of Admiral Parker's voyage to Brazil, printed in 1629, there is a chart entitled, *Description of the West Indies*, in which the new continent is *not* called America. And in a map found in the edition of Mercator of 1632, the southern part is designated as *Peruana*.

The priority of Columbus's discovery is established, too, by a production entitled, *Descriptio Insularum Indiæ Occidentalis*.

## CHAPTER VI.

Canovai, unable to conceal the weakness of his arguments, seeks at last to persuade us that Columbus was the *navigator of Isabella, and Vespucius of Ferdinand!* that is, that the former, protected by the queen, was hated by the king, while the latter was the king's favorite mariner! — an hypothesis quite sufficient to convince us of his own blindness.[1] For if Vespucius was peculiarly the king's man, and was by him employed in the prosecution of voyages, on his own account and unknown to his consort, as Canovai says, how did it happen that, one year after the death of Isabella, which took place in 1504, the Florentine navigator found himself reduced to the necessity of asking the protection of the Genoese, "because he was unfortunate"? To sustain this supposition, Canovai again loses himself in a mass of contradictions. He pretends that *the Castilians alone had the right of going to America;* but he does not note that Columbus and Vespucius were

[1] "The epitaph which Ferdinand caused to be composed for the tomb of Columbus," says the author of a work called, *Patria di Colombo*, "is sufficient to justify the conduct of the king towards this great man." See Cancellieri, Dissertazioni, p. 114.

neither of them Castilians, and that Juan de la Cosa was a Biscayan! If, too, Castilians only could be rightfully employed, how was it that the queen patronized Columbus; and how could the king himself, who was by law debarred from sending his own subjects, have taken Vespucius into his service? In order to get out of this difficulty, Canovai imagines that to the last mentioned navigator secret instructions were given by Ferdinand, to the effect that *all noise and publicity were to be avoided, as well as every exhibition of pomp in imposing names on the lands he should discover.* But he forgets that this passage, or rather extraordinary supposition, is in manifest contradiction to what is previously maintained by him in respect to the pretended letters patent of the king to Vespucius, bestowing on the continent the name of America in honor of him. By a new contradiction, too, he here accuses Columbus of designating as he saw fit the lands discovered by him.[1] But this and other contradictions cost Canovai nothing; for if in this place he draws a feeble portrait of Ferdinand, representing him as employing Vespucius secretly, by and by, when it suits him, he will tell us quite the contrary, affirming that his will was absolute and despotic, and that he made no scruple of *prohibiting the intolerable Columbus.*[2] And then again, in a little while, he will forget also this assertion, to fall into yet another contradiction,

[1] Canovai, p. 256. [2] Ibid. p. 291.

to wit, that *the remarkable privileges of Columbus* bore a prohibition most positive against all which could prejudice discoveries *already made.*[1] The reasoning, then, contained in his justificatory dissertation, being founded on such a multitude of erroneous hypotheses, which both history and authentic documents contradict, falls of itself before the authorities we have cited and the critical observations we have made.

Having thus expressed ourselves in a general manner, in regard to the work of Canovai, and in accordance with suggestions growing out of it, we will now quote certain passages from that of Bartolozzi, which confirm a fundamental remark made by us when speaking of the former, to wit, that the author, so far from succeeding in his attempt to vindicate Vespucius, and prove the genuineness of his narratives, has only furnished fresh arguments against him and his letters, laying open at the same time a wider field for a more substantial refutation of his panegyrists.

Bartolozzi, without relaxing his efforts in defence of Vespucius, does not deny to Columbus the glory of having first discovered the New Continent. He not only proves that Canovai trusted too implicitly to the Cosmography of Sebastian Munster, but he points out the mistakes of this cosmographer himself. He demonstrates that a passage in the work of the

[1] Canovai, p. 324.

latter was mutilated by Canovai, for the purpose of bestowing an originality which did not belong to it,[1] and for the sake of advancing a proposition truly unique, — that Vespucius accompanied Columbus in 1492, — an assertion most palpably false.[2] And he further explains how Canovai's mutilating process was extended even to the narration of Vespucius himself,[3] in order to sustain Munster's error, whereby the truth of history was so much the more violated, that Vespucius is proved to have been in Florence the year of Columbus's departure (1492,) by his own documents deposited in the archives of that city, and examined by Bartolozzi himself, who thus brings to light the double mistake both of Munster and Canovai.[4] He exposes, besides, the anachronism the latter author was guilty of respecting the voyage attributed to Vespucius in 1497,[5] proving at the same time how completely ignorant he was of ancient geographical maps. But although in this regard he shows a better and more extensive knowledge than the author of the Florentine's eulogium could boast,[6] nevertheless, it is evident that he, in his turn, knew nothing about the earliest maps of the sixteenth century. Bartolozzi, in a word, demonstrates the errors which Canovai committed in his calculations of longi-

1 Bartolozzi, p. 90. 2 Ibid. 3 Ibid.

4 Ibid. to p. 100. 5 Ibid. pp. 96, 97.

6 Ibid. p. 102, et seqq., in which he discusses this matter and exposes the errors of Vespucius, Munster, and Canovai.

tude, &c., and that he did not comprehend even those of Vespucius. And it is not a matter of astonishment, therefore, after the exposure of facts we have made, that his work in favor of the Florentine made not the slightest impression on those authors who, since 1788, have treated of that navigator, and that it in no way modified the opinions of Camus, Fleurieu, Peuchet, Muñoz, Malte-Brun, the learned Cancellieri,[1] Bossi, Lanzi, Mariano Llorente,[2] and a host of other writers, from whose works we have quoted, nor yet that it failed to affect the conclusions arrived at by the laborious author of the *Historical Library*, Meusel, who, speaking of the works relating to Columbus, says: "Although the nautical expedition of Christopher Columbus, undertaken for the sake of searching for unknown lands, had a multitude of witnesses, and it is not to be doubted that he was the first discoverer, not only of the islands, but also of the main land of America; *nevertheless, the glory of this great exploit was all but taken from him, and certainly rendered dubious, by the iniquity and foolhardiness of Vespucius, carried to an extent almost unheard of.* This glory, therefore, Tozius has successfully vindicated for Columbus, following

[1] This savant, noted for his erudition, calls Canovai's eulogy of Vespucius *most ingenious*, and ironically declares he will appropriate it to Columbus. His irony is particularly seen at page 257.

[2] Mariano Llorente, *Saggio Apologetico degli Storici e Conquistatori Spagnuoli dell' America*, a refutation published at Florence in 1796, and at Naples in the same year.

others in so doing, who incidentally have attempted the same work." And then, quoting the writings of Vespucius, and referring to Bandini's production, the same author remarks:[1] "Vespucius, when he says that he saw the American Continent as early as 1497, is guilty of an impudent falsehood, for his first voyage thither was in the year 1499, while Columbus had reached it in his third voyage, in 1498; nay, had *seen* the continent (namely, the coast of Paria,) though without landing, in 1495; as it is proved by many writers, notwithstanding what is said to the contrary by the partisans and defenders of Vespucius."

And, indeed, how could any one be either persuaded or convinced by a work, in which there is a constant recurrence of paradox, partiality, and error?[2]

It is fairly proved, then, that the documents produced by Canovai, so far from deserving to be con-

[1] Meusel, *Bibliotheca Historica*, vol. iii. pp. 263, 264. The author, citing the work of Bandini in favor of Vespucius, after having said that it is nothing but an apology, concludes with these words: "*The worthlessness of which work both Tozius and Tiraboschi have sufficiently demonstrated.*"

[2] Canovai was already known for his paradoxes and disputatious spirit, even previously to the publication of his panegyric on Vespucius, as can be ascertained by his quarrel touching the theatre of the Greeks. See the seventh volume of Saverio Mattei's work, Naples edition, page 216. He is reproached with exaggeration, with having confounded actors and philosophers together, tragic with comic poets, and with having had no acquaintance with Greek or Roman legislation upon the subject of theatrical performers.

sidered as recent publications, did really make their appearance forty-seven years before the time to which he refers them, and that, moreover, they were altered and mutilated by him, to serve as a support to a work, of which the learned, and all such as engage, with such marked success, at the present day, in geographical studies, are quite capable of appreciating at its exact value. Equally well has it been shown, too, that the most authentic documents, the most precious, and those which in importance surpass all others known up to the present moment, are such as have lately been published from the archives of Seville and Simancas.[1]

Having thus demonstrated that the production of Canovai cannot, and should not, be regarded as an authority in the question under consideration, the discussion obliges us to return once more to the works of those authors who were contemporaries of Vespucius.

The letters of this Florentine navigator concerning his earliest pretended discoveries were not inserted in the most ancient collection of voyages, called *Libretto di tutte le Navigazioni de' Rè di Spagna colle Isole e Terre nuovamente trovati*, (which was published at Venice in 1504,) notwithstanding the dates of his four fictitious voyages were anterior to that of this publication. It seems then extraordinary

1 See Navarrete, vol. iii., and Bulletin of the Geographical Society, February, 1837, pp. 98, 99.

that, this collection having been printed in Venice, where recent discoveries were universally known, there should have appeared in it not one of Vespucius's letters, nor the slightest mention of any of his fabulous discoveries, when, at the same time, the letters of Columbus, and the voyages of Alonzo el Negro and of Vicente Tañez Pinzon, are duly presented. And this omission should surprise us the more, because *Angelo Trivigiano*, secretary to the Venetian embassy in Spain, who was indefatigable in spreading the news of geographical discoveries in Italy, exercised a great influence upon the publication of the said collection. Besides, if Trivigiano had the like influence on yet another collection, published in 1507 at Vicenza, under the false title of, *Paesi novamente retrovati et Novo Mondo da Alberico Vesputio, Fiorentino, intitulato*, our astonishment should increase at not only finding no letters of Vespucius in the former one, nor any mention of his voyages, but also at seeing in this second his letter to the Medici, touching his expedition, placed after the voyage of Gama, and the discoveries made by order of the Infant Don Henry, after those of Columbus, and even those of Cabral.

Thus the silence observed in regard to Vespucius in the first of these collections, and the order of insertion which marks his Medicean letter in the second, do they not, to a certain point, seem to demonstrate that the best instructed and most impartial of Vespucius's contemporaries, did not admit the pretended priority of his discoveries?

Moreover, this last collection, attributed to Francanzano, was edited, not by Montalboddo, but by Alessandro Lorzi, a skilful cosmographer and chart-designer at Venice,[1] a particular which gives additional weight to our observation. And, indeed, who could have been better informed as to the reality of facts, than a Venetian envoy, resident in Spain at the time of the supposed discoveries; and who could have more easily arrived at the best sources of truth, than an expert Venetian cosmographer such as was Lorzi? And should not these observations render us desirous of knowing why the latter did not insert the letter of Vespucius in advance of the discoveries of Columbus, Gama, and Cabral? Supposing, however, our inability to resolve this problem, if we take for granted that a Venetian agent, residing in Spain at the time, had great influence over the publication of these two collections, and that he was seconded in the work by an expert cosmographer, then it appears to us perfectly logical to conclude that they did not admit the priority of Vespucius's voyages and pretended discoveries; and this with so much the more reason, because, according to what is found in a copy of *Mondo Novo* in the Magliabecchi Library, it is proved that Bartholomew Columbus, who was at Rome in 1505, (two years, that is, pre-

[1] Observations of Baldelli, il Millone, vol. i. p. 32.

viously to the publication of the second collection,) presented a narrative of his brother's first voyage to a prebendary of Saint John of Lateran, who afterwards gave it to *this same Alessandro Lorzi at Venice, he being his friend and the compiler of the collection.*[1] Besides, it is no less worthy of remark that Richaumer, in a German translation of the Vicenza collection, (published in 1508, and, in the opinion of the illustrious Humboldt, more correct and better digested than the *Itinerarium Portugallensium,*)[2] does not say that the new regions were discovered by Vespucius, though such is the announcement in the title of the original. He then did not allow himself to be deceived by the title-page, nor did he admit the claims of the Florentine.

To Peter Martyr, a contemporary historian who lived in Spain, it may be objected that he was very partially disposed towards Vespucius's discoveries, and the passages in his writings touching this subject, which we will again refer to, do not appear to us of sufficiently decisive a character to dissipate all our doubts. For, on the one hand, he was not in Spain when Vespucius pretends he was in the Portuguese king's service, having gone to Venice in 1501, and left that city in October of the same year to proceed to Alexandria, where he did not arrive till three months later, on account of continual disasters he

[1] See M. de Humboldt, Examen Critique, vol. iv. p. 8.
[2] Ibid. vol. iv. p. 87.

encountered by sea. Then, too, he remained a long time in Egypt, prosecuting the difficult negotiation with which he had been charged.[1] And, on the other hand, notwithstanding his merit, he is accused of levity by an eminent contemporary authority, Las Casas, from whom no one can justly withhold the credit of the highest excellence, and still less of a profound and extensive knowledge of facts and events relating to the voyages and discoveries made in his time.

Las Casas, when speaking of the earliest authors who treated of the discoveries made upon the New Continent, says, "that, of all of them, he who was the most worthy of credit was Peter Martyr, by whom the *Decades* were written in the Latin language, he being at the time in Castile; for whatever he there relates respecting the discoveries, was recorded in accordance with the accounts given by the Admiral himself, who made the first discovery, and with whom he often conversed. *But as to all the rest, which concerns the continuance and prosecution of discoveries in the Indies, some false statements are to be found in the Decades.*"

Now this passage is, in our opinion, of great importance, inasmuch as it shows the impartiality of Las Casas, who can in no way be accused of ill will

[1] See Peter Martyr d'Anghiera (*or* Angleria,) Legationis Babylonicæ, lib. iii., appended to his work *De Rebus Oceanicis et Novo Orbe.*

towards Peter Martyr. He apprizes us that this author is exact in all which relates to Columbus and his discoveries, and even assures us that, in this part of the history of the New Continent, he is more trustworthy than any other writer, but at the same time he warns us that these *Decades* are the reverse of true when discoursing upon other navigators. Let, then, this passage of Las Casas, just cited, be compared to what he elsewhere says of Vespucius, and it will be perceived that it also refers to that which Peter Martyr had observed respecting the Florentine navigator; for, if it were otherwise, and if this writer had deserved, in the eyes of the learned bishop of Chiapa, the same credence when speaking of the said navigator as when he spoke of Columbus, Las Casas would not have treated Vespucius as an impostor, and tried to refute his narratives; nor would he have undertaken the defence of the great Genoese with such ardor as to declare that those who pretended to give the glory of having discovered the islands and the main land to any other than the admiral, not only were guilty of injustice, but even offended the Deity himself.[1]

Navarrete also calls our attention "to the deplorable fact that so learned a man as Peter Martyr, and one so fond of writing, should have been negligent to the extent of never rectifying his narrative

[1] See Hist. de las Indias, by Las Casas, a manuscript belonging to the Library of M. Ternaux.

or correcting what he had produced." And Muñoz, before him, had already expressed the same opinion, counselling a prudent reserve in the perusal of his works, in order to escape the errors and equivocations consequent upon the author's heedlessness.

As a proof of his irregularity, where facts are concerned, we will add that he does not mention the death of Columbus till six or seven years subsequent to that event; and that of his account of the conversation he had with the bishop of Burgos, in which the latter showed him a Portuguese chart, said to have been made by a very skilful Florentine, named Americus Vespucius,[1] who, in his expeditions, had passed the equinoctial line, &c.; if this be regarded as an important consideration in favor of Vespucius, then we remark, as a fact not less worthy of attention, that on a cautious examination, such as is recommended by Las Casas, Muñoz, and Navarrete, it still leaves us in doubt. For if, in truth, Peter Martyr had had no doubt as to the pretended discoveries of Vespucius, why did he say "*a chart said to have been made*," &c.? From which it would appear, that neither he nor the bishop had attained that degree of certainty which places a thing beyond doubt. Moreover, if it is established that the Flor-

[1] . . . . . "One of which was drawn by the Portuguese, wherein had been employed the hand of Americus Vespucius, a Florentine, skilled in this art, who had navigated the antarctic regions under the auspices and in the pay of the Portuguese, penetrating several degrees beyond the equinoctial line." Peter Martyr, Dec. II. lib. x. p. 199.

entine navigator always signed the charts he drew, ought we to admit that the one under consideration was made by him, when his signature was not attached to it?[1]

Peter Martyr, too, resided in Spain, knew Vespucius, was member of the Tribunal of the Indies, and ought by consequence to have been able to recognize the handwriting of the Florentine, and his manner of designing maps. Why, then, did he not perceive that the one shown him by the bishop of Burgos was his workmanship, instead of attributing it to him hypothetically? And may it not have been that, confiding in the ability of the supposed author, he gave to him the credit of all the discoveries set down in this Portuguese map, although they had been made by other navigators? In addition to this, does not the *narrative of* André Corsal, in Ramusio, show that geographical charts were already customarily sent from Portugal to Rome before the year 1515? And that Corsal told Giuliano de' Medici that the position of Taprobane must have become known to him by aid of the *marine chart* which Michaël da Sylva, the Portuguese ambassador, carried with him to the Holy City? Which fact proves that marine charts, confirmatory of discoveries, were officially sent to ambassadors from Portugal, and that the Court of Lisbon made no mystery of them; for Cor-

[1] On this subject see the work of Tray Pedro Simon, *Noticias Historicas*, chap. vi. and vii.

sal's expressions convince one that the examination and knowledge of such documents were refused to nobody that had any interest in consulting them.

Now, as this same system of communication was observed by the court of Portugal towards that of Spain, is it not possible that the Portuguese map in question, shown by the bishop of Burgos to Peter Martyr, and *supposed* to have been drawn by Vespucius, was rather the work of Portuguese navigators, just as were those which Corsal says were sent into Italy?[1]

Let this be as it may, however, Peter Martyr is not considered as an infallible authority, except when writing of Columbus; and Las Casas, that celebrated historian, who was not only his contemporary, but also a witness of most of the events of the time, does not regard him as worthy of credit when treating of other navigators. He not merely passes upon him the impartial judgment above recorded, but he lived long enough to protest against the name of *America*, given to the New Continent in the work of Ilacomilus, published in Lorraine,[2] and in other productions

[1] If Vespucius had been recognized as a learned cosmographer at the time when the New Continent was first discovered, and if he had become somewhat celebrated previously to the first voyages of Columbus, would Queen Isabella, in her letter of September 5, 1493, (see Navarrete, vol. ii. Doc. 71,) to Columbus, recommending him to choose a good cosmographer, have pointed out Antonio de Marchena?

[2] See Hist. de las Indias, vol. i. chap. 140, MS. of the Library of M. Ternaux.

printed elsewhere than in Spain. In a word, he critically examined the dates of discoveries and the relations of navigators, in order to prove, that priority in the discovery of the New Continent belonged to Columbus, and that the name of America fixed on that part of the globe was a usurpation. "Here," says he, "is the place to hold up to view the injury and injustice done by this Americus Vespucius to the Admiral, by arrogating to himself the discovery of the main land, and by calling it after his own name alone. Whence it arises that foreigners, who write upon the Indies in the Latin or their vernacular tongue, and who design and fabricate charts and maps of the world, denominate them *America*, just as if they had been sought out and found by the said Americus."[1] And, again, the words of the same author are, "But this we affirm, that the Admiral was the first who discovered the main land of Paria. Hojeda was the first after the Admiral, and with Hojeda was Americus. The Admiral left San Lucar the 30th of May, 1498, and Hojeda and Americus sailed only the following year, 1499."[2] And to this we will add, that though in certain details the learned historian of the Indies may have committed some faults, as Navarrete says he has, yet is he worthy of

[1] MS. of the Historia de las Indias, by Las Casas, chap. 148, (same library.) "*By that which Americus wrote, to obtain a name, and to appropriate, by tacit usurpation, the discovery of Terra Firma.*"

[2] See Las Casas, Hist. de las Indias, MS., chap. 164, (same library.)

belief in all which pertains to pretended priority in the case of Vespucius's expeditions and discoveries.

Navarrete, who beyond a doubt is one of the most weighty authorities in such matters, acknowledges that Las Casas is always an erudite and truthful writer, and meriting the greatest respect, except when engaged on his favorite theme and ruling notion, the manner of establishing dominion over the New Continent; and it follows, therefore, that, in all matters relating to Vespucius, he is more deserving of confidence than Peter Martyr.

If Vespucius, and the claims made in his behalf by panegyrists, are to be judged according to the accounts of these two contemporary historians, Peter Martyr and Las Casas, the testimony of the latter, learned as he was, must be rejected before a favorable conclusion can be come to, even as it regards the intentions alone of the Florentine navigator. But ought such testimony to be entirely rejected? We think not. And, indeed, it is impossible to refuse the evidence of an historian living at the time, personally acquainted with the navigators, and having in his possession documents of the two brothers, Christopher and Bartholomew Columbus, written with their own hands. We will in another place call attention to the silence which is observed as to Vespucius's fabulous discoveries, by another historian, also contemporary, whose relations respecting Columbus have furnished valuable materials for the history of the New World's discovery, — the famous *Bernaldez*, curate of Los Palacios.[1] To the said discovery this author devotes a long chapter,[2] which is headed, *How the Indies were discovered*, and not how *America* was,[3] and the sole subject discussed in it is Columbus, who is extolled for his vast acquirements in cosmography, for what he *had read in Ptolemy* and other books, and especially for his profound knowledge of John de Mandeville's writings.

From the silence of Bernaldez as to Vespucius's would-be discoveries, it may at least be concluded that the Florentine's voyages were insignificant as compared to those of Columbus and other navigators, since they did not seem worthy of mention to an author, who yet was so well informed as to Columbus, that he even cites by name the works which powerfully influenced the mind of that great man. And this silence is the more remarkable, because we are assured by Bernaldez *that he habitually set down in his books the facts as fast as they happened.*[4] But, then, how did it happen that his work, which was finished in 1513, contains no notice of the Florentine's feigned discoveries, notwithstanding the numerous publications in which they had already been

[1] *Memorias de los Reyes Catolicos*, a manuscript in M. Ternaux's Library. It is in folio, and contains 246 chapters. Bernaldez, in these memoirs, recounts a great number of events that happened in his time, that is from 1450 to 1513.

[2] Memorias, chap. 118, p. 372.

[3] Bernaldez, MS.

[4] Bernaldez, Memorias, chap. 158.

proclaimed? To this let it be added, that not a single document can be found to prove that Vespucius was invited to Lisbon by the Portuguese sovereign, but that, on the contrary, it is an established fact that Columbus was thus invited by John II. of Portugal.[1] And herein may there not have been another mystification, either on the part of Vespucius himself, or of the editors of the letters attributed to him, whereby what was true of the Admiral is put down to his account?

We will indicate yet another singular coincidence which exists between what Vespucius says and what Las Casas recounts.[2]

The former, in one of his letters, asserts that he had given to king Emmanuel, of Portugal, a book, containing a narrative of his voyage, *which book was lost.*[3] And the latter tells us, that when Columbus left Barcelona he deposited with the king, to be kept in the royal archives, *a little book*, in which were recorded his expeditions and discoveries, — another instance, very possibly, of the same juggle or confusion, by which what indubitably belonged to Columbus was appropriated by Vespucius. And have we

[1] Letter, dated 20th March, 1488, in Navarrete, vol. ii. p. 5. Vespucius says that when at Seville, he was sent for by the king of Portugal. The letter also from John II. to Columbus, is also addressed to the Admiral, who was then at Seville: — *To Christopher Columbus, our special friend, in Seville.*

[2] Historia de las Indias, chap. 83.

[3] See preceding remarks in this work.

not, at least, a right to surmise this, when, in the invaluable work of M. de Humboldt, we see it demonstrated, by comparing the text of the first voyage of Vespucius with that of the first voyage of Hojeda,[1] that, though the latter is attributed to the Florentine, they are one and the same, but narrated by Vespucius, who added a description of the manners and customs of the aborigines, according to the custom of navigators of the sixteenth century? The second voyage, too, of this Florentine, is it not almost identical in reality with that of Vicente Yañez Pinzon?[2]

We are willing to admit that the letters and narratives imputed to Vespucius were in fact written by him; but, after this discussion, what ought to be said as to the materials out of which they were made? Should we not conclude that, though Vespucius was the recorder, the discoveries, and the groundwork of what he relates, belong to the voyages of Hojeda and Pinzon, and that he did nothing but give an account of them in his letters to the Medici[3] and to

1 See Examen Critique, vol. iv. p. 95, et seqq.

2 Ibid. p. 200, et seqq.

3 We have already essayed the identification of this personage. Now let it be supposed that it was Lorenzo di Pier Francesco de' Medici, indicated by Bandini. He was born in 1463, and was very celebrated for his learning. This author says he had been ambassador in France in the time of Charles VIII. But, unfortunately for the hypothesis, he died at the beginning of 1503, and the narrative of the third of Vespucius's pretended voyages, which is supposed to have been addressed to him, was written subsequently to the fourth expedition of 1504. Now, Vespucius arrived at Lisbon, according to his own account, the 18th or 28th of June, 1504, that is, nearly a year and a half

Soderini, insinuating, however, in certain passages, that he took an important share in them, or rather assuming the entire merit of them to himself?[1]

His famous letter dated at Çape Vert, the 4th of June, 1501, found by the Count Baldelli Boni,[2] which has been adduced in evidence of his good faith, presents an additional argument to strengthen what we have advanced, as well as what Las Casas asserts. We have already shown that the documents pertaining to Vespucius which have reached us, offer every characteristic of having been forged, or, to say the least, of being doubtful as to their genuineness; and a healthy criticism demands the greatest circumspection and the most conscientiously severe examination of manuscripts, before admitting such in evidence. It is requisite, therefore, palæographically to scrutinize the epoch at which the original of the production in question was digested, to ascertain whether the handwriting be authentic or that of a mere copyist of later date, whether there be any interpolations, and, in a word, what, if any, marks of fraud are to be found. These observations are not

after the death of the Medici, and it is not at all likely that, when such a long time had elapsed after the decease of a personage as highly distinguished in politics as in literature, the Italian *savants* at Lisbon should have known nothing of it.

[1] *It is the astronomer of the expedition who thus speaks, wholly puffed up with the secret he fancied he possessed of determining the longitude*, &c. &c. See Humboldt's Examen Critique, vol. iv. p. 182.

[2] Il Millone of Marco Polo, by Count Baldelli Boni.

made with any idea of regarding the document we are considering, in a spirit of narrow prejudice; for the *savant* who discovered it in the manuscript of Pietro Voglienti, would not have given publicity to it if he had been of our opinion as to its character. Nevertheless, supposing it to be genuine, we will say in the words of M. de Humboldt,[1] *that in every thing which concerns the Florentine navigator there is a sort of fatality mixed up with documents the most authentic, for the express purpose, as it were, of creating confusion.* And as to this letter of Vespucius, which some would avail themselves of to decide in a positive manner respecting his third voyage, and to prove that he had passed the fiftieth degree of south latitude, we will remark, that it is by no means exempt from the same anomalies and serious difficulties which have been pointed out by critics in his other epistles previously published in collections of voyages and in Bandini's work.

Here, for example, is a passage intricate to the last degree, and not susceptible of any satisfactory explanation: — "After twenty days of navigation, from the time of quitting Cape Vert, having made nearly seven hundred leagues, I landed where the inhabitants were *white. It was a part of the same territory which I had discovered* for the king of Castile,[2] as in a previous letter I have already said, *but*

[1] Examen Critique, vol. v. p. 166.

[2] Note to the same, vol. v. p. 32. Brazil is mentioned in Pinzon's and Vespucius's voyage of 1499 and 1500.

*it is further to the east.*" Now, on the one hand, if it be Brazil of which he here speaks, the aborigines of that country were not *white;*[1] and, on the other, how is it to be decided what this land is, east of that which Pinzon had discovered? Here, again, Vespucius takes to himself the credit of the last mentioned navigator's discovery, saying, without the least reserve, *the same land which I discovered*, when he could have seen it only in the preceding voyage, under the command of Pinzon; and yet he declares the land was found by himself for the king of Castile! What reliance, then, can be placed either in his honesty of intention or in what he states, when he does not so much as allude to Pinzon or the expedition in which he beheld the said land, but, on the contrary, assumes to himself the title of discoverer?

The letter in question, moreover, exhibits, like his others, an immense number of errors upon the latitudes noted, as well as upon the distances run; and the nomenclature of the principal factories (*comptoirs*) of India, which would have added a great deal to its interest, he had from some one employed in the Portuguese marine. This same nomenclature, it should be observed, was preceded by another, likewise Portuguese, and yet antecedent to the letters of Vespucius, which was found in the chart-book of Vasco da Gama's voyage in 1497, the manuscript of which has recently been met with in Portugal.

[1] Examen Critique, vol. v. p. 38, note second.

Another observation, important, though in a different sense, as it regards this letter, is that the illustrious author of the *Examen Critique*, after having cited Navarrete's conclusions upon Vespucius's third voyage, (the final words of which are these: "*Vespucius cannot be named as having discovered the lands*, — the southern part of the New World, — *and as having been the first to enter the seas beyond the tropic of Capricorn.*" [1]) adds, — "I perfectly agree with M. de Navarrete in this opinion; nay, I think it is in my power to fortify it with arguments," etc.

Now, if Vespucius did not go beyond the tropic, that is, if it be admitted that he went no further than the twenty-third degree of south latitude, it follows that neither he nor his narratives supplied the geographical elements with which Beneventano and Cotta were furnished, which are found in the Ptolemy of 1508, and which we have above cited, being the same which provided those editors with the following note: — "The Portuguese mariners examined this portion of this land, as high up as the fiftieth degree of south latitude; but yet they did not arrive at its southern extremity." It follows, also, that the Florentine, not having got further than the tropic of Capricorn, could not have encountered floating ice. So that every conjecture founded on the suppo-

[1] *Examen Critique*, vol. i. pp. 71 & 72; and Navarrete, vol. iii. pp. 318, 320.

sition that he approached the pole, is deprived of support.

This famous letter, too, proves more strongly than any other, the presumptuous silliness of its author, the contempt he entertained for other navigators, and how, in extolling himself to his friends and countrymen living abroad he took their credulity by surprise, and led them to believe that he was *the man* of discoveries, the most learned of cosmographers, and the greatest savant of his time. In it, when speaking of his rencounter with Cabral's vessels which had arrived from India, he begins by expressing his regret that the mariners on board of the two vessels there anchored were able to give him so little instruction, *because there was not a single cosmographer or mathematician in either of them, which was a great mistake.* But this mistake, our cosmographer proposes to remedy by *introducing in the narrative given to him by these marines, certain corrections in accordance with the cosmography of Ptolemy!* And, not satisfied with this piece of pedantry, he first enumerates the many countries which the vessels he met with at Cape Vert had visited, to wit, the Cape of Good Hope, Sofala, Mozambique, Quiloa, Mombaza, Melinda, Magadoxo, Dabul, Albarcorne near Cape Guardafui, the Red Sea, Moca, Malacca, Ceylon, and Sumatra; and then he thus speaks: — "I have, besides, myself the hope of seeing and visiting in my turn, during the voyage in which I am now engaged, most of the places which I have just mentioned." After having suffered this slight escape of jealousy against the navigators of his day to take place, he more fully develops his entire thought in the following passages: — "*I will even discover more*, of which on my return I will write a good and true account." . . . "It is," says he, speaking of longitudes, "an arduous task in a widely different sense, and *one which few persons understand, except those who can deny themselves sleep.*" . . . . "*For the sake of these resolves, I have often sacrificed my slumber, and my life I have shortened by ten years; a sacrifice which,* IN THE HOPE OF OBTAINING A RENOWN WHICH SHALL LAST FOR AGES, *I do not regret,*" etc.

The passages found in this letter of Vespucius, when compared with what we have already analyzed of his in this work, appear to justify the assertions of Las Casas; and, in truth, the words of the Florentine unveil his inmost thought, which profoundly manifests the desire of making himself the monopolist of discoveries. If other navigators had visited lands never seen by him, little value had their discoveries in his eyes; because, forsooth, they had no cosmographer or mathematician to describe them, or, in other words, because he himself had not been of their party. Not only does he never praise any contemporary navigator, but he even abstains from mentioning one of them by name. Thus, in the letter so often referred to, he might have spoken of Cabral; but no, he says nothing of him. He minutely relates, that the two vessels he encountered at Cape Vert were on their return from the East Indies, and that they had formed part of the fleet of thirteen vessels sent to Calicut (Madras) fourteen months before. He could not, consequently, have been ignorant that they had belonged to the fleet commanded by Cabral, who the preceding year discovered Brazil. And, therefore, nothing was more natural for him, had he acted in good faith, than, when transmitting all these details, to add, *one of the thirteen vessels sent to Calicut fourteen months ago*, and belonging to the fleet commanded by Cabral, who had discovered the land, or at least landed on it, etc. For it is to be presumed that, having left Lisbon, as he says he did, the 13th of May, 1501, when everybody in Portugal already was informed of Cabral's discovery of Brazil, he could not but have been aware of the same, and of the Admiral's name who was the author of it.[1] Ac-

[1] We must here remark, in spite of the coincidence of the departure and return of Vespucius in this voyage (as set down in the *Quatuor Navigationes* of Ilacomilus) with the departure and return of an expedition cited by Antonio Galvao, in a work called *Tratado dos Descobrimentos*, — that this author of the sixteenth century, when speaking of an expedition composed of three vessels, from Lisbon in May, 1501, says not a word of Vespucius. Consequently, although there is this coincidence of dates, there is no confirmation, by this author, of Vespucius's voyage, while the discovery of Cabral is perfectly well established.

counts of this discovery had been brought to Lisbon, by a Captain Gaspar de Lemos, whom Cabral sent from Brazil in the early part of May, 1500; so that Vespucius must necessarily have known of it on his departure, which took place a year later. But he invariably affects a complete ignorance of all that other navigators had done before him.

Now, we wish to ask those who sustain this Florentine in his honesty of purpose, and pretend that his intentions in regard to Columbus's discoveries were pure, saying that he never designed the appropriation of these to himself, how it happens that the name of Columbus is never found in all his letters but once, and that only when he speaks of Antillia? Is it probable, that in 1501 he knew nothing of that admiral's three voyages already accomplished, nor of his having discovered the main land? He assigns him but a poor part in the work of discovery; and in the single instance where he mentions his name, it is not with the slightest reference to his grand discovery of Terra Firma, although he must have very well known that Paria had been found by him. Why, then, did he speak of him only once, and that in relation to an island?

It may be objected, that had the Florentine been bent on despoiling the Genoese of his glory, he would not have written with the looseness which is perceptible in his letters. And it is even pretended that these *were never intended for publication.* But need any one be told that it is by secret means that good faith is the most easily surprised, and that clandestine communications and notes never destined for publicity, are the instruments where with vast intrigues are digested and prepared? And was not such a thing the most to be apprehended at an epoch when discussion did not prevail, and when, as Bossi most truly observes, charlatans and impostors abounded?

A like argument, then, can in no way whatever justify Vespucius; and particularly as no one can affirm that his letters were not intended for publication; but, on the contrary, it is adverse to him, seeing that they were given to the public during his lifetime. For, in fact, the letter of his we have been speaking of, first appeared in 1504, and then again in 1505, with this title: — *De Ora Antarctica per Regem Portugalliæ pridem inventa, impressum Argentine, per Mathiam Hupfuff.* In 1506 it was printed in German, and in 1507 it was found in the collection of Vicenza. During the same year (1507) it was presented in the famous *Cosmographiæ Introductio* of Ilacomilus, together with an account of the four pretended voyages of the Florentine. In 1508, his letters came forth to the world once more, in a collection called, *Paesi novamente retrovati*, etc., published at Vicenza, and also in the *Itinerarium Portugallensium*, of Madrignano. In 1509, too, they were inserted in the *Cosmographiæ Introductio*, published at Strasburg, by

Gruninger; and in 1510 there was a letter from the press of Tritemio, entitled, *The Globe laid out on a plain surface, with islands and regions newly discovered by Americus Vespucius, of Spain.*

Now, Vespucius died the 22d of February, 1512, and if he had not intended that his letters to his friends should be published, he would without doubt have disavowed such publicity, for he had plenty of time in which to do it. But, instead of this, inasmuch as there existed relations between him and the inventor of the name of America, that is, Ilacomilus, he indirectly consented to the injustice committed against Columbus, in the same way as he had approved of the publication of his letters.[1]

It has been attempted, too, to construct an argument in favor of Vespucius, from the fact that at the time of the Admiral's death, an account of the pretended third voyage of the Florentine had been printed, which treated of the two preceding ones. But it is sufficient, in our opinion, to meet this, that the name of *America* not having been imposed during the lifetime of Columbus, the Admiral could not complain of the flagrant wrong done to his righteous claims. And, indeed, what offence could he have taken at the publication of Vespucius's first voyage, that is, the one made under the command of Hojeda,

[1] On the relations which existed between Vespucius and Ilacomilus by Lorraine, see a note by M. de Humboldt, in the Bulletin of the Geographical Society, vol. iv. p. 412, second series.

when this captain did not go to the new continent till subsequently to himself? Did he not know that such a publication could do no harm to his glory; since it was impossible for him to foresee that facts would be falsified after his death?

Another argument which may be adduced in support of Vespucius's having landed in Brazil, is a certain passage in the relation of *Empoli*, in Ramusio; but should it not weigh seriously on every opinion formed at Florence and elsewhere in his favor, the effect produced by the correspondence of his compatriots established in Spain and Portugal, who, through national partiality, would try to persuade those to whom they wrote that Vespucius had played an important part in discovery? And does not the history of discoveries of all sorts, even in our days, prove how disputatiously every nation claims priority for those who belong to it?

It must be observed that Empoli was, like Vespucius, a Florentine, and that the vessel in which he sailed, though forming part of the Portuguese fleet, had been armed by the Marchionis, Florentine merchants established in Lisbon. It is to be presumed, then, that such persons, whether doing business in Lisbon or Seville, actuated by a sentiment far from being unworthy if just, were well disposed to claim for their countryman a great portion of fame, in opposition to that acquired by the great Genoese. And it should be recollected that, at the time of which we speak, the rivalries of the Italian republics were not yet at an end.

Be this as it may, however, if Empoli in his narrative, when speaking of Vespucius, says that the expedition, in which he was himself, landed on the same continent previously discovered by that navigator, this passage, supposing it not to be a later interpolation in the text of the copy published by Ramusio several years after it was written,[1] cannot call in doubt the priority in discovery of the southern part of the New Continent by Pinzon, Lepe, and Cabral, even admitting the genuineness of Ramusio's publication. In fact, it is incredible that Empoli, who sailed from Lisbon the 6th of April, 1503, in the expedition of Alphonso de Albuquerque, could have been ignorant of the discovery of Brazil by Cabral three years before. For how is it possible that, being on board of a Portuguese fleet, he could remain unaware that the land he was visiting had been found out by a Portuguese Admiral at a time so little remote from that of his own landing? Does not the very name of *Vera Cruz* which he gives to Brazil, prove that he knew this land had been discovered by Cabral, since it was Cabral who thus called it from the moment he first saw it?

1 Has it not been seen that modern sites, of which the latitude and longitude were supposed to be known, have been interpolated in the tables of Ptolemy, and inscribed on charts drawn by this geographer of Alexandria?

If this passage of Empoli's be compared with others contained in the letters of Pascoaligo, Venetian ambassador at Lisbon, and with another of the Venetian Domenico Cretico, neither of whom attributes to Vespucius the discovery in question, must not what he says be regarded as very suspicious? It is certainly much less worthy of credit than the testimony of two official agents of the Venetian republic, both of them contemporaries, added to the demonstrated fact that the said discovery was made by Cabral. So that we do not hesitate to believe that an impartial criticism will admit the authenticity of passages found in the Venetian agents' documents, since they correspond with facts, rather than of a faulty statement in the account of Empoli, who, to secure the glory of an Italian, said nothing of Pinzon, Lepe, or Cabral.

Yet a third argument, brought forward in vindication of Vespucius's intentions, is, that if he had himself contributed to impose his name on the New Continent, Ferdinand Columbus, so jealous of his father's fame, would, without doubt, have complained of it, and so much the more, as he finished his book in 1533. And this, negative argument as it is, has some importance, though it is far from furnishing any satisfactory proof of Vespucius's honesty of purpose. For, in the first place, Ferdinand Columbus's book has not reached us in the original, but only in a Spanish retranslation, by Barcia, from an Italian version of it by Alonso de Ulloa. Then Las Casas, who produced it anew, almost word for word, treats Vespucius as an impostor, notwithstanding its author makes no reproach against him. And, moreover, in the year 1533, when this work of Ferdinand Columbus's was terminated, the name of Americus Vespucius had not generally been admitted into chartography, that is, priority in the discovery of the New Continent was invariably assigned to the Admiral in all geographical charts up to 1520 ; and it was only in one found in the *Solinus* of Camers, published in this year, that the great discoverer's son could have possibly seen for the first time the name of America applied to the western world. But, connected with this name, he must also have found a note, attributing to his father the earliest discovery of that vast continent, in these words : *Acting under the orders of the king of Castile, Columbus, a Genoese, discovered this land and the adjacent islands in the year* 1497.

It is very likely, too, that Ferdinand Columbus knew nothing of this chart of the *Solinus* of Camers ; and besides it, no other one, that we are aware of, with the name of *America* upon it, was published between 1520 and 1533, — the year when his work was finished. Consequently he could have been acquainted with but a single one bearing this denomination, — a denomination, moreover, very far from being clear and definite, for to it is attached the word *Province*, nor is it applied to the *whole* of the immense continent. Added to which, in juxtaposition, is the above remarkable note, establishing his great father's prior right to discovery, a circumstance greatly calculated to palliate the painful impression which must have been produced upon his mind by the chart in question, if in fact it ever fell under his notice.

But, however this may be, we are inclined to believe that the silence of Ferdinand Columbus in respect to Vespucius, of which some would avail themselves for the latter's justification, is in no way decisive and will profit nothing, especially as he likewise observed great circumspection and reserve on other matters of vast importance, which must have been known to him, such as, for example, his family and the country which gave his father birth. He limits himself to telling what other people's opinions were, but his own he says nothing about.

## CHAPTER VII.

We will now proceed to make some remarks upon the nature of the arguments adduced by the partisans of Vespucius, which may be of service in enlightening the mind of the reader. Robertson disputes the truth of the Florentine navigator's narratives, on the ground of Oviedo the historian's never making mention of him. But from this silence others have arrived at a directly opposite conclusion, pretending that Oviedo, being hostile to the Admiral, was not unwilling thus tacitly to confirm the claims of Vespucius. So much liberty, then, being taken by others in the way of interpretation, for the sake of drawing foregone conclusions, we too, in our turn, propose to add a remark or two in the matter.

The probability is that Oviedo was indisposed to mention Vespucius's pretended discoveries, because he would not violate the truth of history, and because he was well aware that nobody in Spain would have believed any thing which could be said in favor of that navigator in direct opposition to an universally acknowledged fact, that is, the first discovery of the New Continent by Columbus. Or, it may be, that the historian's guarded reserve as to the Florentine and his affairs, proves that in Spain no account whatever was made of one or the other, and that even when attention happened to be turned in the direction of foreign publications respecting them, it was only for the purpose of refuting the claims of Vespucius and his panegyrists, as was done by that great historian Las Casas.

Among these conjectures the reader will select that which best pleases him. The first and the second we have cited to show how difficult, if not impossible, has become the task of justifying Vespucius for those who praise him. It has also been attempted to draw a conclusion favorable to his rectitude of purpose, from a few commendatory words found in Ramusio. But this author's eulogium is, in our opinion, quite inadequate to the vindication of the Florentine's motives, and much less is it capable of giving to his narratives the impress of truth.

Ramusio was indeed the most learned compiler of his age, but he never had submitted to his inspection the documents we are acquainted with, nor did he ever discuss the questions which the moderns have raised respecting the Florentine navigator and his fabulous expeditions. In addition to which, he was an Italian, and we do not think that his panegyric upon *the extraordinary intellect and splendid genius of the excellent seignior Americus*, can reduce to a nullity what is said against Vespucius by Las Casas, Schoner,[1] and Herrera.

[1] The astronomer Schoner makes known his suspicions of the fraud

Moreover, the work of Las Casas, wherein there is question of Vespucius, the invaluable *History of the Indies*, had not then, nor has it even yet, been published. Ramusio, therefore, was unacquainted with the objections which authorities like Las Casas, and after him other learned Spaniards, have made to the tenor of Vespucius's narrations, and even to the honesty of his intentions. So that an impartial critic will allow more weight to the words of the latter than to those of the former, whose laudatory

practised by Vespucius. See a little geographical work of *Joannis Schonerii, Carolostadi Opusculum Geographicum, ex diversorum Libris et Chartis Collectum.* Nuremburg, 1533, ch. xx. and xxi., and sect. xi. His testimony respecting Vespucius is very important, notwithstanding the errors of his systematic geography. Born in 1477, he died in 1547. He filled a mathematical chair at Nuremburg. His astronomical tables, which were published after those of Regiomontanus, and which were called *Resolutæ*, because of their perspicuity, made for him a celebrated name. He wrote a mass of works, some of which are in the Royal Library of Paris. His little geographical treatise (*Opusculum Geographicum*) he composed according to the books and charts of his time, at which epoch he could already appreciate the question pertaining to the name imposed upon the New Continent, and equally well could he foresee the great injustice thereby done in defiance of the evidence of facts and the rights of Columbus.

It is not, however, these two contemporaries of Vespucius alone, Schoner and Las Casas, and Herrera besides, (whose sources of information, too, were authentic,) that accuse that navigator; but to those writers already cited by us, we must add others still who decide against him and his claims, such as Mosquera de Varumbo, Numantina, ch. x. fol. 74; Malvenda, ch. xvi.; Charles Etienne, in his Dictionary, word *America;* Solorzana, *De Indiarum Jure*, etc. lib. i. c. 4; L'Evêque, in his works, *passim;* Fr. Antonio de la Calanca, Chronic. de Santo Agustinho nel Perv. Book i. ch. iv. fol. 28; Father Manoel de la Vega, in his work, *Historia del Descobrimiento de la America por Cristobal Colon.*

assertions in regard to the Florentine, we will maintain, are of less importance in the present discussion even than the statements of Herrera.

We are perfectly aware of the attempt to undervalue the accusations contained in these statements, so hostile to Vespucius, on the ground that Herrera's Décades, not having appeared till towards the beginning of the seventeenth century, are outside of that limit within which the opinions of the learned are worthy of consideration as materials for critical history. And it is indeed true that, according to the rules of such history, the importance of an historian's assertions, who was not contemporary of the facts he reports, becomes proportionally less, while he himself can never occupy the same place as another not laboring under this disadvantage; but it is likewise true, that this rule can at no time be admitted to the fullest extent, without risking the rejection of very many works, which constitute the authenticity of history, although often both written and published several centuries subsequently to the events they describe. Should many passages, and facts in great number detailed by Heroditus, Strabo, Pliny the elder, and other authors of antiquity, he refused as worthless, because these authors were not actual witnesses of what they relate? Most assuredly not. Herrera then ought to be ranked among the historians of the sixteenth century, although his work was not published till the year 1601; since his information was obtained from sources purely authentic and antecedent to that epoch, for which reason his opinion in the case of Vespucius is very conclusive. And if it be necessary to reject him as an authority on account of his having lived and written only during the latter portion of the century of discoveries, how can the historians and critics of the nineteenth century, who have engaged in this debate, and who have more than two hundred years of separation between them and Herrera, venture to constitute themselves as authorities in a discussion so important? But we think that a careful examination of this learned writer's works will suffice to convince every one that, if his statements ought not to command the same confidence as those of Las Casas, they should, at least, occupy the very next place after them on the score of historic value. For the truth is, that this laborious writer accomplished a mass of works which demonstrate the vast extent of his information respecting the affairs and events that occurred in his time. And even to the present day[1] he has always been regarded as one of the best, most conscientious, and most impartial of Spanish histo-

[1] It was only the paradoxical Canovai that attacked Herrera; but this celebrated historian found at Florence a savant whose defence of him was unanswerable. See Mariano Llorente, Saggio Apologetico degli Storici e Conquistatori Spagnuoli dell' America, Florence, 1796, *passim*. Prescott's Ferdinand and Isabella, vol. iii. p. 56. London 1838.

rians.[1] His history enjoyed the rare privilege of being declared official by a decree of the Council of State, and what he says, therefore, upon the subject before us should be received as genuine.

Yet another argument brought to aid the cause of Vespucius is, that, in the famous process of the exchequer against Columbus, to which all contemporary navigators were cited to depose in opposition to the Admiral, he himself was not called upon, nor were those books which had been published in foreign countries respecting him, made any use of in the preparatory judicial informations. But to this it may be replied, either that the exchequer did not require him to make his deposition in the matter, because it regarded him as a party interested, and therefore liable to suspicion, (which according to every rule and law of jurisprudence must have nullified the whole procedure,) or, that, he never having made the discoveries treated of in the works published abroad, and never having been the first to find out *Paria*, the exchequer or attorney-general

[1] M. de Humboldt, Examen Critique, vol i. p. 297, recognizes the authority of Herrera in these words: "Two works, *the authority of which cannot be called in question, the Décades of Antonio de Herrera, and the Manuscript of Pigafelta.*" And if the authority of Herrera cannot be called in question as to Martin de Behain, a navigator who preceded Vespucius, how can it be when Vespucius himself is concerned? Indeed, if Herrera had, without doubt, the original notes of the pilot of Magellan's expedition before his eyes, how can it be suspected that he was not exceedingly well informed as to the Florentine's discoveries?

saw fit, leaving him aside, to demand the presence, as witnesses, only of such navigators as had visited the countries in question, and were, therefore, better able than Vespucius to ascertain the exact period when the discovery of Terra Firma took place. To which we will add that, whatever might have been the exchequer's acquaintance with books upon Vespucius's discoveries, printed in Italy, Lorraine, and other foreign countries, it was impossible to admit them as legal evidence, (they not being Spanish publications,) in a process conducted within the kingdom of Spain, and according to the national code of procedure; consequently, it should in no way surprise us that not the slightest attention was paid to them.[1] And the exclusion of Vespucius from this process, during the whole of which his name is only once mentioned, and that with the modest title of *pilot* annexed to it, proves nothing definitely, except it be that all eyes in Spain were fixed upon the grand and noble figure of Columbus, upon the man whose genius had brought to light a New World!

To show how free from guile was the Florentine navigator, it has been further argued that he always had the notion of arriving in Asia, when on his voy-

[1] In the reign of Ferdinand and Isabella jurisprudence in Spain underwent a great reform. The laws were executed with severe impartiality, and even the tribunals were newly organized and a new code published.

age to the new continent, and that this fact alone ought to convince us that the discovery of the said continent did not enter into his views.[1] But it must be observed, that at the time of this famous discovery it was the common belief of all navigators that the newly-found continent made part of Asia, — an error in systematic geography which for a long time afterward prevailed, but which, nevertheless, did not prevent these same navigators from believing, and publicly proclaiming in their works, that they had discovered countries never visited by any one before.

Then again, how could any one have expected to find in the letters of Vespucius, written during the lifetime of Columbus, that this land ought to be called by his name? There are many things a man suffers to be divined, which he dares not put on paper; he delights to see them adroitly managed and published by others, but from touching them himself he carefully refrains. Yet, be this as it may, there is not less truth in the assertion that, even while Vespucius believed the new continent to be only a portion of Asia, he was equally convinced that his expeditions to the New World were real discoveries. The mere quotation of his words is quite sufficient, in our eyes, to substantiate what we have said; and we would only call to mind

[1] Canovai, the great panegyrist of Vespucius, has drawn a conclusion altogether contrary to the expressions of the navigator himself, when he says that he had discovered *a great deal of Terra Firma, and islands without number.*

the single passage in which, speaking of a Portuguese expedition to Africa, he says, — *A voyage like that I do not call a discovery.* [1] In his second expedition, he pretends that he discovered *a boundless territory ;*

[1] The learned Portuguese geometrician, Pedro Nunes, demonstrated in his book, *Defensam da Carta de Mariar*, that the discoveries of islands and main lands by the Portuguese were made on a scientific system, and that no navigator ever left Portugal without being well instructed in astronomy and geometry, and well furnished with suitable instruments. (See a memoir, by the author, upon the scientific acquirements of John de Castro, *Bulletin of the Geographical Society*, vol. x. p. 220.)

The Portuguese expeditions, therefore, were profoundly calculated, and scientifically directed, according to the principles of cosmography and geography. (See Ribeiro, Memoirs of the Royal Academy of Sciences at Lisbon, vol. viii. p. 169.)

The accusations of Vespucius against Portuguese navigators are unjust, and show how, on every occasion, his jealousy of them leaked out. According to many documents, and accounts of contemporary authors, it is manifest that the Portuguese government determined the fitting out of expeditions consonant to ideas and plans previously arranged and known. And, in fact, if we go as far back in search of scientific projects as to the establishment of the famous Nautical Academy of Sagres, long before the birth of Vespucius, it will be seen that, even supposing him to have been in the Portuguese service, this Florentine did no more than execute, under a Portuguese commander, designs purely Portuguese.

M. Ranke has lately found in the Archives of Venice, a letter which proves that, even previously to Columbus's voyage to Honduras and Veragua, in the month of October, 1501, *it was already known in Portugal, that territories to the north covered with snow and ice, were contiguous to the Antilles, and to the land of the Perroquets, newly discovered.* This land is situated near Brazil. (See this passage in the *Examen Critique* of M. de Humboldt, vol. iv. p. 262.)

Now, this curious document shows that, in Portugal, the information on so grave and important a point was excellent, and that the communications and geographical *data* could not have been furnished to the court of Lisbon by Vespucius, since he did not return till the elsewhere, he calls this territory a *new world*, and adds, *Three ships are fitting out for me here, that I may go on a new voyage of discovery.*

Thus, on bringing these, and a great number of other passages, previously cited, into one view, and on examining the whole discussion at once, it will be perceived that the words *discoprire* and *Mundo Nuovo*, which Vespucius employs, ought not to prove beyond dispute the sincerity of his intentions. On the contrary, his expressions seem intended to persuade those persons to whom his letters were ad-

following year. (1502.) And, too, the fact we are going to state proves that the said court was under no necessity of inviting him in 1501, (as he pretends,) for the sake of finding out new countries, after the discovery made by Cabral. Scarcely had King John II. learned the discovery of Columbus, when he commissioned the Count d'Abrantes, in 1493, (*the same year,*) to examine the new countries thus found. (See Barros, decade i. book iii. ch. 2, and Humboldt, *Examen Critique*, vol. v. p. 96.) Examine, also, the letter addressed to the Cardinal, Archbishop of Porto, published by Pedro Affonso Malheiro. In the work of Father Manoel de la Vega, (*Historia del Descobrimiento de la America Septentrional,*) published for the first time in Mexico, in 1826, by Bustamente, — the author, speaking of Columbus's third voyage, (1498,) says it was that navigator's intention to sail toward the south, beyond the equinoctial line, and thence to go west, so as to ascertain *if King John of Portugal was mistaken in affirming that there was terra firma at the south.* Even before this sovereign's accession to the throne, his father, Alphonso V. had consulted a famous Florentine astronomer, Toscanelli, (1474,) as to a western passage to *the land where the spices grow.* And in the letter of the latter we have a proof that the Portuguese were occupied with a western passage to the Indies more than twenty years before the discovery of America. Already, too, previously to 1464, John Vaz Cortereal, accompanied by Alonzo Martins Homem, discovered the land of *Bacalhaos*. (See Memoirs of the Royal Academy of Sciences at Lisbon, vol. viii. p. 309.)

dressed that he had really discovered new lands, or, in one word, a new world.

Thus, we have gone through with the examination and discussion of all the arguments brought forward in vindication of Vespucius's honesty of purpose, and to them we have opposed our own; from all which we think it results, that the former are *not beyond the reach of attack*, and, by consequence, are a failure; and, moreover, that an irresistible fatality seems to attend every attempt to sustain the honesty of that navigator. The feebleness, too, of all that has been adduced in his behalf, as shown in what has gone before, serves but to augment the fame of Columbus's genius, and to paint in still stronger colors the flagrant injustice committed against that great man.

But all that has been, or that may be, said about the intentions of Vespucius, notwithstanding its importance, as relating to the knavery of having fixed his name on a portion of the globe discovered by Columbus, must be regarded as matter of a very secondary nature; since the fundamental point in dispute is, not what he meant or did not mean, but whether he did or did not discover any part of the new continent. Neither does the matter in hand require demonstration of his having been engaged in navigation, but it does of his having ever discovered any thing by himself, — of his having been the first to fall upon any one point of the new continent in an expedition under his direction and command, as was the case with Columbus, Pinzon, Lepe, Cabral, Hojeda, and others.

Now, if it be admitted, in accordance with documents genuine beyond a question, that Columbus before all others discovered the new continent, (that is, the islands and Terra Firma,) as Pinzon did also a portion of it, that Hojeda visited Venezuela, that Lepe coasted along the shore south of the equator, that Cabral first saw and landed in Brazil,[1] and that Coelho was the earliest discoverer of another part of this vast country; if, too, it cannot be denied that Vespucius's first voyage, the one he made under Hojeda's command, together with his two following fictitious expeditions, bear a most striking likeness to those of Pinzon and Hojeda, while his fourth resembles that of Coelho;[2] if all this be as we have

[1] Not only do none of the Portuguese historians of the sixteenth century mention Vespucius, as we have said elsewhere, but the king, Emmanuel, in his letter dated at Santarem, July 29th, 1501, to the sovereigns of Spain, communicating to them Cabral's discovery, says not a word of him.

[2] We will here transcribe several very remarkable passages from the Examen Critique of M. de Humboldt, (vol. v. pp. 211, 212.) After having displayed a profound and vast erudition, and discussed the narratives of Vespucius, comparing them with the accounts of voyages by other navigators above mentioned, this savant concludes in these terms; — "Considering the disjointed and extremely disorderly condition in which Vespucius's letters have reached us, it is difficult to decide which were the several Spanish and Portuguese expeditions to which he was successively attached," etc. etc. . . . "It appears to me probable, that his first voyage was made with Hojeda,

said, does there not arise from this mass of indisputable *data*, unanswerable evidence of abominable wrong done not only to Columbus, but likewise to other leading navigators of the time in which Vespucius lived? Indeed, if Brazil had been seen by Pinzon, and then by Lepe in January of 1500, afterwards by Alonzo de Mendoza, and in April of the same year by Cabral, *whose discovery, at least, is a historic truth*, and if, on the other hand, Vespucius never went to this country in command of an expedition, how can he possibly be ranked among the discoverers of the new continent? To say that he could be, would involve the most flagrant of contradictions.

It has been said that Vespucius in Pinzon's expedition saw a portion of the new Southern Continent before ever Cabral beheld it. But granting this to be true, he must have seen it only as others in the same fleet saw it, and the meanest sailor of them all had as much a right to claim the discovery as he. No, the glory of the enterprise belonged, not to him, but to his commander. And this is so true that Juan de la Cosa, his fellow voyager, did not say in his famous chart, *This cape was discovered by Vespucius*, but, quite the contrary, for instead of even so much as referring to him by name, he confirms

his second with Vicente Yañes Pinzon, and his fourth with Gonçalo Coelho. But under what chief his third took place, we are as yet in ignorance."

Pinzon's discovery in the note which we will transcribe anew, — *This cape was discovered in the year* 1499, *for Castile, Vicente Annes* (Pinzon) *being the discoverer.* He puts beyond doubt also the fact, that the island of Ferdinand de Noronha was for the first time seen by a Portuguese expedition of which Vespucius did not form a part.

The Florentine's admirers presume to assert that his memory ought to be held in reverence, because he was so expert and clever; but we are not disposed to concede that, on such grounds, either justice or impartiality requires us, going upon conjecture opposed to fact, to raise a monument to him for achievements belonging to other persons. And when it is said that severity of judgment in respect to him does not become us, and those who, like us, class him among the lowest of navigators at the great epoch of discoveries, because, forsooth, he was a skilful cosmographer! We reply, — granting he was all that, so likewise was Strabo, so was Ptolemy, and so were many others before him, skilful in a very different sense from that in which he was, and yet they never usurped the glory of another.

It is well worthy of remark, too, notwithstanding the immense fame his partisans would claim for him, that in 1512 (and this date is very important,) his charts were of so little authority in Spain, that the main map of André de Morales was the only one recognized by the government as exact, and the only one which was in great repute.

But then, say some, Vespucius's descriptions of savage manners and customs are well and amusingly written; but so also, we answer, are certain narratives of the same sort, found in different coast-accounts given by pilots, whose names are hardly known. Yet the question returns upon us, not whether he was a good cosmographer or an agreeable narrator, but whether he was the discoverer it is pretended he was. And before a learned and impartial criticism his claims must fall to the ground.

In a single word, the brief and true statement of the case is this: the grand discoveries made by Columbus, Hojeda, Pinzon, Lepe, Cabral, and Coelho,[1] were real discoveries, confirmed and established by genuine proofs. *Their dates rest on docu-*

[1] Claude Bartholomeo, in his *Orbis Maritimus*, assures us that Vespucius, in his voyage of 1501, discovered the *Rio de la Plata*, of which there is not the least probability. And notwithstanding it has been supposed that this navigator reached the fifty-second degree of south latitude, a conjecture adopted by Mr. Southey, in his *History of Brazil*, there is not the slightest likelihood of its being true. One single remark is quite sufficient, in our eyes, to show how little confidence should be placed in a portion of Vespucius's narrative, touching this pretended discovery, which is, the profound silence observed in regard to it by all Spanish and Portuguese writers. For it is not credible that an expedition so adventurous and bold as the discovery of a river, (which was made by *Solis* in the year 1515,) should have remained unknown to Coelho in 1503, had it previously taken place.

Again, the return of Gonçalo Coelho to Lisbon with two ships which had escaped being wrecked, gives a direct contradiction to what Vespucius says in his second letter about the captain's death and his own arrival at Lisbon in command of the two vessels. Had it been so, how was it that all his contemporaries knew nothing of the fact?

*ments sure and certain*, as M. de Humboldt truly observes; while the dates in Vespucius's pretended discoveries are deserving of no confidence whatever, and are in contradiction with each other.[1] In all material respects, as it has been remarked, the voyages of Vespucius and Hojeda correspond, but in the account of the former the narrative is confused, the succession of events is changed,[2] and from the beginning to the end of it the reader is filled with perplexity,[3] and almost despair.[4] His astronomical dates, too, which belong to the voyage he made with Hojeda, are mixed up with his recital of that in which he accompanied Pinzon.[5] So that every impartial person, who has followed us thus far, must acknowledge how difficult, if not impossible, it is to concede to Vespucius's relations the reputation of authenticity, and will plainly perceive how all

[1] See Examen Critique.

[2] See Ibid.

[3] Ibid. vol. iv. p. 82. "I can in no way explain," says the author, "Vespucius's dogmatical and confused description, except by the very common phenomenon of a *halo*," &c.

[4] See Ibid. vol. iv. p. 168. Where speaking of Vespucius's letter dated at Lisbon, the author says: "Why did he confide to Benvenuto a letter addressed to the king of Portugal?" Which unaccountable circumstance we point out for the sake of designating another strange peculiarity in the Florentine's narrative.

[5] "An astronomical date," remarks M. Humboldt, "the conjunction of the Moon and Mars, (August 23, 1499,) mixed up with the recital of Pinzon's voyage, when it doubtless belongs to that of Hojeda, offers a very weighty, if not insurmountable, difficulty. Could it have got from one voyage to the other by accident? Besides, it is not referred to in the *Quatuor Navigationes*, but is alone found in Vespucius's letter to Lorenzo de' Medici."

attempts made by his eulogists in his behalf have hitherto failed.

Columbus, and other navigators above enumerated, have on their side facts, and authentic documents and records to support these facts; but as for Vespucius, facts, documents, records, and even the reasoning built upon these, all tell to his disadvantage, and only serve to set in a more frightful point of view the gross iniquity committed against the first great discoverer of the New World, and the far-famed mariners who were his immediate successors in the glorious work.

END.

www.ingramcontent.com/pod-product-compliance
Lightning Source LLC
LaVergne TN
LVHW011204110826
845150LV00006B/1317

* 9 7 8 1 4 2 5 5 1 8 8 9 9 *